One of the most important components of raising emotionally and spiritually healthy kids is to create a family environment that is filled with love and joy. In *The Rhythm of Home*, Chris and Jenni have given us a guidebook on how to cultivate a family culture where our kids can grow and thrive. If you are searching for guidance on how to forge healthy, deep relationships with your children that will last a lifetime, then this is the book you have been waiting for.

MELANIE SHANKLE, *New York Times* bestselling author

This is not a book of to-do lists but a warm invitation to consider how you can intentionally cultivate the home you truly want your family to flourish in. Chris and Jenni do that beautifully with simple rhythms and invite you to join them on the journey of creating the space where children are cherished and enjoyed, know they are deeply loved, and love coming home to.

JOHN AND STASI ELDREDGE, *New York Times* bestselling authors of *Wild at Heart* and *Captivating*

What I love about this book is the fact that it isn't just a concept that sounds good in theory; it is a practical, valuable approach that the Graebes share from experience. I've had the benefit of knowing their family outside of the book, and they're the kind of people you'd love to learn from. These words are your chance to do just that and to benefit from the patterns that shape our days. This book is approachable but also meaningful and Christ-centered. I'm happy to put my name alongside theirs, and I know you'll want to do the same as you read!

ANGIE SMITH, author of *Se*

Wow. If only this book had been published a decade ago—it would've saved us years of trial and error! This isn't your typical "how-to" parenting book—it's a manual on how to establish healthy habits for a vibrant family life. A must-read for anyone who wants to take their family to the next level.

JASON AND TORI BENHAM, entrepreneurs, speakers, authors of the bestselling marriage book *Beauty in Battle*

A book about how to do family life in the twenty-first century is certainly timely and necessary. Chris and Jenni have lived the highs and lows of family life and share them with us in this book. It will leave you with practical tools and loads of hope to build a healthy, godly home. The stories and examples will give you hope, warm your heart, and show you ways to be a healthy family, no matter how difficult the culture may be. If your family feels broken or dysfunctional, or you just need some help getting through the daily grind of life together, you will find the help you're looking for in *The Rhythm of Home.*

ANNE BEILER, author and motivational speaker, founder of Auntie Anne's Pretzels

I can't think of a better couple to write this beautiful book. As a mama to five boys, two of whom are now in college, I can testify to how quickly the years fly by, and how vital it is to be intentional with the foundation we lay and the time we have! The five practices found in *The Rhythm of Home* are a trustworthy road map to follow for creating the thriving family culture you desire.

JEANNIE CUNNION, author of *Mom Set Free*

For anyone who has never met Chris and Jenni Graebe and their wonderful family, you are in for a treat. They will warm your heart, stimulate your thinking, and inspire you as parents. *The Rhythm of Home* has the heartbeat of God to help us all rethink and reimagine what our own home could be. Their style is invitational, never with the taint of guilt or shame. The stories from their lives help us grab hold of the truths they share. With each chapter, the family map unfolds, leading us to the treasure of our own home and what we want it to be. Enjoy this new best book on the family.

MARK AND JAN FOREMAN, authors of *Never Say No*

This book is a *must-read* in the day we live in, teaching us to center our hearts on God and others. The rhythms and intentional practices taught in it are what make where we live not just a house but a life-giving, thriving *home*.

MESHALI MITCHELL, acclaimed photographer, visual storyteller, faith-based speaker, podcaster

In life, we are unavoidably shaped by the unseen yet powerful rhythms that surround us. We might not always have a say in the circumstances and situations that impact our days, but we can choose the rhythms that inform our vision, our responses, and even our peace. Chris and Jenni are terrific guides to help us navigate and choose purposeful rhythms for our family. In this excellent book, they creatively offer hands-on, tried-and-tested tips to life-affirming practices, all from a place of honesty, insight, compassion, and love—the cornerstones of their own home and relationships.

KAY WYMA, writer, podcaster, author of *The Peace Project*

I've had the privilege of getting to see Chris and Jenni live this book out in the way that they steward and savor their family with such grace and intentionality. This book is brimming with wisdom and go-to rhythms that are approachable and attainable. How I wish that I had had this beautiful resource when I first embarked on parenthood! The life-giving truths and practices shared here are bound to reap a harvest in your family for years to come.

CHRISTY NOCKELS, singer, songwriter, author of *The Life You Long For*

Chris and Jenni have given us all a beautiful reminder of the remarkable gift it truly is to be a family. With grace and wisdom, *The Rhythm of Home* will ground you in the true purpose of parenting—to love and shape these incredible humans God has entrusted you with through the habits that fill your home. A must-read for any parent!

WILLIE AND KORIE ROBERTSON, stars of *Duck Dynasty*

CHRIS & JENNI GRAEBE

THE RHYTHM OF HOME

FIVE INTENTIONAL PRACTICES FOR A THRIVING FAMILY CULTURE

A NavPress resource published in alliance
with Tyndale House Publishers

NavPress.com

The Team:
David Zimmerman, Publisher; Caitlyn Carlson, Acquisitions Editor; Elizabeth Schroll, Copyeditor; Olivia Eldredge, Managing Editor; Julie Chen, Designer

For information about special discounts for bulk purchases, please contact Tyndale House Publishers at csresponse@tyndale.com, or call 1-855-277-9400.

ISBN 978-1-64158-292-6

Printed in the United States of America

30	29	28	27	26	25	24
7	6	5	4	3	2	1

To the incredible collective village that raised us:

To Jenni's family: Steve, Tricia, and brother Wes

To Chris's family: Rob, Mary, and brother Eric

And to the incredible men and women God invited into the collective village that walked with us from childhood to adulthood. Who chose, for reasons we will never truly understand, to see something special within us, and to pour their lives out for us, praying, uplifting, and consistently pointing out the best in us. Steering us ever onward toward our true home, our Savior.

Being shaped and molded over the years by phenomenal people such as you is one of the greatest gifts of our lives. It is a blessing we pray our own kids will experience.

We stand on your shoulders today.

CONTENTS

THE SACRED JOURNEY OF PARENTING

May you have the eyes to see
That no visitor arrives without a gift
And no guest leaves without a blessing.
JOHN O'DONOHUE

Take hold of the life that is truly life.
1 TIMOTHY 6:19

CHRIS

There are a handful of moments in your life that seem to stop time altogether—that somehow mark you forever and set your life in a new direction.

I experienced one of those time-stopping moments at the age of twenty-one. I was enjoying an ordinary Sunday at church when the pastor stepped up to the platform and said the words that would change my life forever: "Turn around and greet your neighbor." I looked behind me to extend the customary handshake of welcome, and life suddenly began moving in slow motion. I'm pretty sure an angelic choir began to sing and turned the heavenly spotlight to shine directly on . . . her.

She was *beautiful*—a stop-you-dead-in-your-tracks kind of beautiful. The kind of girl I'd only ever imagined meeting. Her name was Jenni. She was breathtaking, and I just couldn't take my eyes off her. Somehow I knew life would never be the same.

At first, we agreed to just be friends, but we quickly realized that wasn't going to last long. After a few months, we snuggled up close on a wooden bench in the courtyard of a hundred-year-old church in our hometown of Franklin, Tennessee, and began the journey of our relationship. We dated for five short months, were engaged for five extra-long months, and then, just five months after that blissful wedding day, we got a big surprise.

I'll never forget the moment it happened. We were visiting Jenni's family for the holidays. I was sitting next to Jenni in the back row of a dark theater, surrounded by my brand-new in-laws, as the opening scenes of *Meet the Fockers* began to play.

Within the first few minutes of the movie, Pam announces to Greg that she's pregnant. "How do you know?" he says. "I'm two weeks late, I'm nauseous, my boobs hurt, and I can smell *everything!*" she replies. Out of the corner of my eye, I saw Jenni freeze, a handful of popcorn suspended in front of her lips. She turned to look at me, eyes wide. For just that second, time stood still once more. She had been mentioning those same symptoms to me for the last few weeks.

Sure enough, the next morning and four tests confirmed it: We were having a baby.

Jenni and I are both adventurers at heart, so at first, it all sounded pretty exciting, honestly. A baby? *Pssh.* How hard could it be? But once the reality began to set in, we started to wonder, *Are we really ready for all this?* Jenni was still finishing up her last year of college. Not exactly perfect timing. We had absolutely no idea what we were doing or what to expect.

I remember anxiously calling one of our mentor couples to seek their wisdom and advice. As always, their encouragement was right on point. "Guys, listen. You're never ready," they assured us over speakerphone as Jenni and I sat on the floor of our living room, staring at each other. "No one is ever completely ready. God is with you. You have what it takes. He's always been with you, and He always will be."

Jenni decided to stick with the plan and finish her last semester of college. Our son was due in mid-August, so we said, "Perfect! He'll pop out right before school starts, and Jenni can head right back to class!"

Our son's due date came and went. Jenni had no choice but to waddle back to class that fall semester still ready to pop. (Her words, not mine!) Finally, the long-awaited day came. Jenni called me from class, saying that early labor had begun during her professor's hermeneutics lecture. (I don't blame you, Kaden. I'd want to get the heck out of that class too, bud.) I raced like a NASCAR driver to the religion building at Belmont University. Jenni's kind classmates brought her out to me, and we headed for the hospital.

And there it was again—the sense that for just this moment, time stood still. I'll never get over the deep sense of awe and wonder that washed over my heart as I watched our son come into the world. Suddenly he was here, our baby boy, our first-born. Nothing could have possibly prepared me for the moment when they placed him in my arms. He was breathtaking, and I just couldn't take my eyes off him. Somehow I knew life would never be the same.

Something had shifted forever. Up until this moment, we had only been investing in a *rhythm of us*, and while our marriage rhythms would still continue to grow, a brand-new rhythm had just entered our lives. Our *rhythm of home* had begun.

Throughout the course of parenting, we experience quite a lot of "I've never done this before." Never experienced this level of sleep deprivation before, never wiped poo off someone else's rear before, never potty trained toddlers before, never had to choose the right elementary school before. As the years go by, we learn from our mistakes as well as from our victories, hoping that by the time the last child hits this or that stage, we'll finally have this whole parenting thing figured out.

Alongside the unparalleled levels of joy we experience as parents come unparalleled feelings of doubt, worry, and fear. Finding our rhythm as a family takes a lot of time, a lot of trial and error, and a lot of leaning on the Lord to guide us. Perfection is never the goal, and it's not even the point. Finding our rhythm of home is about being deeply connected as a family—filling our life together with the intentional rhythms that will lead us all to grow closer to God and to each other. It's about crafting a vision that will serve as a guide, a framework to hold on to when we find ourselves in one of those inevitable "We've never been here before" moments. Our rhythm of home can help us navigate all the twists and turns that come our way on this journey called family.

It's not an accident that you and your family were placed in your home together. The Lord specifically chose to bring you all together for a purpose. Each person in your home is unique, with specific giftings and personalities they bring to the family table. Each one matters. Developing a rhythm for your home is about coming together to establish values and visions as a collective family unit.

God's vision for our families is greater than we could ever possibly imagine. *That* vision is what we chase after: His voice, His plan, and His purpose for our family. *His* rhythm for our home.

> Each person in your home is unique, with specific giftings and personalities they bring to the family table. Each one matters.

JENNI ——————————————————

As a young girl in college, I kept two pictures scotch-taped to the dashboard of my white Mustang convertible. Every time I glanced down at the dash to check the gas gauge or signal for a left turn, there they were, staring back at me. One was a scene of a boy kneeling before a girl, asking her to marry him. The other was of a group of little siblings, smiling and laughing and playing together on a sunlit playground. There was no such thing as Pinterest way back then. No Instagram or social media (if you can even imagine such archaic times). These visuals I'd clipped from a good old-fashioned magazine and taped to the front of my dash were my attempt to capture the specific stirrings of my heart for the season ahead. Cheesy, I know, but amid all the life-altering choices that lay before me as a young twentysomething, I knew I needed to lean on the Lord to guide me: I wanted to keep these visions continually before my eyes as a daily reminder to pray for the pieces of the future I longed for.

Fast-forward a couple of decades, and here I find myself smack in the middle of that young girl's dreams. Nearly twenty years in, happily married to my very best friend, with five precious children under our roof, deep in the golden years of marriage and family. This beautiful life God has blessed us with has absolutely blown every expectation I ever had for my future, exceeding every dream I ever imagined while driving around the back roads of Nashville all those years ago. I'm so grateful for every minute of it, and yet, like any parent, my days in this season look very full. The to-do list waiting for me as I wake up each morning never seems to run out. Around every corner there are always mouths to feed, heads to brush, clothes to fold, events and games to rush to, outcomes and hopes to pray for, and meaningful moments to savor. And underlying it all: a home, a life, and an incredible family to love, nurture, and grow.

Parenting, as many have said, will be the hardest yet most exhilarating thing you will ever do. And, I would also add, parenting is one of the most formative, meaningful roles of your life. I have had many roles over the years—daughter, student, friend, singer, wife, pastor, writer—and all have changed me in some way or another, but nothing has shaped me more than being a parent. As theologian Wendy M. Wright says: "If there ever was a school of love, it is the family—a school not simply in the sense of an environment where information is passed on but an environment that profoundly forms us."[1]

The gift of this life together is one of the greatest blessings I've ever experienced. And yet, as I'm guessing you may have discovered along the way as well, dreaming of and praying for your future marriage and family is a lot easier than living out the daily work required to bring those dreams of a thriving family to life. Like anything of great worth and value, building a family and cultivating a thriving home takes a lot of thought, hard work, and intentionality.

What Chris and I both discovered throughout those early years of family life is that we won't get there by accident. We don't just drift our way into the life we long for. Building a healthy home requires developing intentional rhythms to guide us as we pursue a thriving family life.

In other words, we need to craft a rule of life for our family.

What is a "rule of life"? Stick with me; it's not as crazy as it sounds. (In our previous book, *The Rhythm of Us*, we explore this idea in relation to marriage. Beginning with your marriage is foundational—a first and important step to building a strong vision for your family is getting on the same page as your spouse.[2])

A rule of life is a simple, helpful tool that absolutely anyone can use. Essentially, the ancient practice of creating a rule of life involves envisioning the person you want to become—spiritually, emotionally, mentally, physically—and then crafting a set of personal life habits that will lead you toward becoming that future person.

For better or worse, we get to choose the rhythms that fill our home. Crafting our family's rule of life is a way to live with intentionality, a way to let our days be formed by the truth of the gospel. Rather than a list of rigid rules to follow, the rhythm we create for our family is more like a trellis supporting the growth of a budding vine. Not restricting us, but continually pointing us toward the *best* way. I love what writer and professor Margaret Guenther says:

> The vine must not be tied too tightly to the trellis, but just snugly enough so that it is supported and free to flourish. Like the vines, we too need to be supported but not constricted, held up but not rendered immobile.[3]

Our rhythm supports intentional growth toward the life we feel called to live as a family. For us, that has meant centering our family practices around the ways of Christ. In fact, the original idea of a rule of life emerged centuries ago out of a desire to organize life around the ways of Christ, based on the understanding that growth toward Him is not only possible but the only true path to flourishing. As we center our family practices around the ways of Christ, we cultivate an environment where growth toward Him and a flourishing family life are possible.

For better or worse, we are all profoundly shaped by the rhythms we grow up in.

The truth is that the rhythms we live from today determine the kind of family we become tomorrow. For better or worse, we are all profoundly shaped by the rhythms we grow up in. Saturday morning pancakes, camping trips in the fall, weekly time around the table. Whether we realize it or not, there is a regular rhythm unfolding every day in our home. The question becomes: "Is this the rhythm we *want* to create?" In other words, will these habits that make up our life together take us where we long to go? Are we creating a thriving family culture through the habits we choose to practice today?

It's never too late to start new family rhythms. While those of us who grew up with unhelpful or even harmful rhythms were of course marked by them, we don't have to remain trapped by them. We get a fresh start. We can actively choose, with the help of a wise and caring community around us, to reject old patterns and establish new, healthier rhythms.

Ultimately, we all want to root our kids and ourselves in a foundational sense of all that is good and right and true—to ensure that when our kids leave our home, they will carry with them a strong sense of love and security and a beautiful picture of the family life we shared. But how do we go about accomplishing that on a practical level? What are the rhythms that will carry us and keep us connected throughout these precious years under one roof?

One of the sweetest ways God has faithfully led me over the years has been by placing along my path older, wiser people just ahead of me on the journey to sit with and learn from. I've come to value seeking them out as often as I can. Ferociously when needed. What I have discovered is that while every family is unique, bringing its own set of personalities and dynamics to the table, the healthiest families seem to share the same basic rhythms. Of course, no single formula can meet everyone's needs, but there are a handful of core practices that *can* benefit anyone: rhythms of a flourishing home we can all practice and pursue.

Throughout this book, our goal is to pull back the curtain and take a deeper look into the rhythms of a vibrant family life. By sharing the trials and triumphs of our own experiences as well as what we've learned from flourishing families around us, we hope to give you some intentional handles to grab on to, a handful of key practices to try out in your own family life.

What we are not attempting to do is cover every single aspect of parenting and family life under the sun, presenting you with a long list of how-tos and schedules to follow. This is in no way an exhaustive parenting manual or an extensive look at eight hundred ways to connect with your kids. With five of our own still under our roof, we are very much right in the thick of family life, in desperate need of learning and practicing these rhythms just as much as anyone. Join us for the journey!

Our hope is to simply walk together through the rhythms that can lead *all of us* toward the thriving family culture we long for.

To fill our homes with the rhythms we value most and to be reminded of what a great gift it truly is to be a family.

To cherish every moment of this wild and precious season when these remarkable humans live under our roof.

It will be over before we know it. Those sticky fingerprints left on the wall, the pitter-patter of little feet coming down the stairs, shooting hoops for hours in the driveway—these will all soon be distant memories. We want to hold on as much as possible to the awe and wonder of these fleeting years, fighting with all we have against the monotony of the mundane that so often veils our eyes from the true sacredness of this season. The time and effort we invest working these healthy rhythms into the fabric of our family will shape each one of us and live on well beyond our years.

We hope this book will serve as a reminder to us all of the inherent sacredness of building a family. A celebration of the great gift of home. A compilation of the very best rhythms that carry us and shape us in the homes we build together. We will never parent perfectly. No one will. But when it's all said and done, we will have had the unbelievable blessing of loving and shaping one another, under the same roof, for this specific amount of time. There will be crazy hard days, without a doubt. Excruciating trials, exhausting nights. Heartbreaking moments, for sure. But we will also experience delights and joys beyond our wildest imaginations. Our hearts will love at levels we never dreamed possible. Our lives will be richer, fuller, and more meaningful than we ever imagined because of the gift of loving these little ones and the blessing of becoming a family. There is nothing like it.

So we invite you to join us as we travel through five intentional rhythms of a thriving home. We pray that as we share these practices that have carried and shaped us, your own unique rhythms will also begin to emerge along the way. Write them down. Talk through them with your spouse and kids.

There are a thousand different ways we could choose to live our life together. Our goal is to intentionally center our days around rhythms that lead us toward loving God and loving each other.

When it's all said and done, what mark will we leave as a family? Did we delight in each other? Speak the words that bring life? Pour ourselves out for those around us? Did we say yes to the great adventures the Lord invited us into and cherish the great gift of life together with the awe and wonder it deserves? May this book remind us all of the remarkable joy of family, of the blessing it is to love and shape each other for this one sweet season. May it give you permission to notice and name what your unique family values most and to build your life around those rhythms.

Here's to the great gift of family.

Here's to celebrating all that is good and meaningful in the time we are given together.

Here's to you. Here's to us.

Here's to the rhythm of home.

PART ONE

THE FAMILY RULE
OF LIFE

AFTER WE HAD OUR THIRD CHILD, I (Jenni) remember feeling a growing frustration at the rapid pace of our life. Rushing from one activity to the next left me feeling too exhausted and hurried to savor any of it. I began to have this sinking feeling that life was slipping right through my fingers.

Up to this point, with the addition of each kid, though it took some time, eventually we had found our rhythm again. But as our family grew and grew, finding our new rhythm as a family was proving harder and harder. What were all those wonderful things we used to love doing together? What was that one super important thing we always used to say? Our life was filled with new levels of joy and meaning from these incredible new blessings, of course, but our increasingly frenzied pace was beginning to take over, leaving us with little energy or space for what we truly valued most.

We began to talk with each other and other parents about the increasing pace of our schedules and our desire to live a slower, more intentional life. We began to take some time to notice and name the rhythms that drew us closer as a family and brought out the best in all of us. A lightbulb went off when we realized we could center our life around those things rather than constantly long for a window to fit them in. We decided to take back our time.

In this section, we'll discover the powerful practice of crafting a rhythm of life for our families. We'll envision the future we want for our families and learn how to cultivate a home and community that support that vision. We'll discover how to create regular rhythms that will help our values sink deeper into our hearts. When we intentionally make space for the rhythms we value most, the results tend to follow.

1

BUILDING YOUR FAMILY TABLE

Starting with a Vision

You will show me the path of life. In your presence is fullness of joy.
PSALM 16:11, WEB

rhythm: a strong, regular, repeated pattern of movement

JENNI

I've always been a sucker for high school graduation pictures. The flash from youth to adulthood gets me every time. But the closer my own kids get to that inevitable season, the more in danger I find myself of tearing up at any given moment. We are just 293 days away from launching our oldest kid out into the world, so in this season of life, nothing melts me faster than all the sweet pictures from families just ahead of us saying goodbye to their graduating seniors.

Graduation is often a time of looking back, of reflecting on the long and short time of childhood, on eighteen years' worth of memories that have led to this one moment. Often graduation events include tables displaying the tangible images of those memories—favorite toys, beloved stuffed animals, tiny stamped footprints and baby rattles, playbills and vinyl records, a pair of old cowboy boots or faded summer-camp T-shirts. I'm always awed at the visual journey through a child's life. At one such event, as I took in each item representing the life of a young person on the brink of adulthood, I heard the Lord whisper, *What's on your table?*

I thought of all the tables I am filling and all the memories I hope to fill them with. When we launch each of our precious kids into the world, what pieces of life will represent their experiences here in our home? What do I hope to find on that table? What do you hope to find on yours?

OUR FUTURE TABLE

Before we can craft a rhythm for our home, we first must envision the kind of family we hope to become. What will the future us look like?

We all have tables we're filling. Our individual table, our marriage table, our family table. Stop for a moment right now, think of your future family table, and write down your vision. Get as specific as you can. Getting specific about our future pulls it out of fantasyland and into an achievable goal. Psychologist and author Dr. Henry Cloud describes crafting a vision as "defining a future that does not yet exist."[1] God gave humans the unique ability to dream and envision a healthy, vibrant, rooted-in-God life, and He partners with us as we journey toward it.

When your friends and family gather to celebrate as you

launch each child into the world, what do you hope to see on that table? When you gather with your adult children and grandchildren someday, what do you hope that experience will be like? What things do you hope will be said of you and your family? What do you dream of for your family life together?

As you seek to build your rhythm of home, to fill your future table, involve your family. Celebrate and consider each family member's strengths, ideas, and uniqueness. Each person deserves a place in your collective rhythm. To help you fill your table, take turns answering the following questions. Each person's vision for the future might be drastically different, and that's okay. As you discuss these questions as a family, you'll likely find areas of overlap across answers. Ground the discussion in the values that are most important for your family. Our kids will be much more excited to participate in bringing the family vision to life if we include them in the brainstorming and honor their thoughts and ideas. Try plotting your answers to the following questions in "Your Future Family Table" below.

> Each person deserves a place in your collective rhythm.

- What are our favorite activities to enjoy as a family?
- What words do we hope others would use to describe our family?
- What kinds of adventures do we want to experience together?
- What values are most important to us?
- Which weekly habits bring you the most joy?
- If you could fill a table with all your favorite memories of home, what would a few of them be?

Your Future Family Table

For better or worse, we get to choose the habits that fill our home. For these few short years that we have with these precious kids under our roof, what rhythms will we teach them? What practices are most important to us? What values will be written on our hearts and in our story? What do we want to invest our time in together? What images of us and our life together do we want to give our kids?

As professor Thomas Howard said:

You are the attendants at this shrine [your home]. See to it that what goes on here is a small picture of what ought to go on everywhere. It doesn't go on everywhere, but your task is to see that it does here. This is the spot allotted to your priesthood. Be faithful.[2]

As we move toward the future we long to cultivate, it's important to remember that life never goes exactly according to plan. There will be plenty of surprises and detours along the way. Keep filling your life with the rhythms you value. Trust the story that God is writing for you and your family. And remember, we are each a work in progress; perfection is unattainable.

> Before we can fill our home with the rhythms we value most, it's important to acknowledge the ruts that hinder us.

Encourage yourself along the way. The fact that you picked up this book tells me you care deeply about your children and the home environment you are raising them in. Our job is not to worry about the results but rather to be faithful in the process. Trust the table that God is filling.

CHRIS ————————————————————————————

All change begins with honesty. Before we can fill our home with the rhythms we value most, it's important to acknowledge the ruts that hinder us. We need to take a good, hard look at the reality of where we currently find ourselves as a family.

If you're anything like me, you might be tempted to assess

your current reality based on where you *hope* it is, or maybe even where it *used* to be, rather than where it *actually* is. The truth is, though, that something shifts within us when we take the time to honestly notice and name what is happening in our life together. Taking a good, long look changes our perspective. Maybe you've been avoiding it, hoping if you ignore it long enough it just might change on its own. But only the truth frees us to walk in a different way (John 8:32). It's time to get brutally honest.

Think through the rhythms in your home. Are there habits that feel particularly heavy or draining? Are there routines that used to work for your family but don't anymore? When we take the time to notice where we've gotten into a rut and work to get out of it, we open up space for more life-giving family rhythms in the future.

Talk through the habits that are a consistent part of your family life. See which ones need to stay and which ones need to go. When we intentionally make room for the rhythms we value most, we move closer to the thriving family culture we long for.

Take some time this week to reflect on (and, if you're married, discuss with your spouse) where you feel you are as a family.

- What does our family table look like in this current season?
- Which rhythms are working well for us?
- Are there habits we've fallen into that we know need to change?

- Which rhythms from our future table are missing from our current table?
- Are there any habits we used to practice that we'd like to make room for?

INHERITED RUTS AND RHYTHMS

When we enter family life, we don't enter alone. We each carry with us a mixed bag of ruts and rhythms from our own years of growing up under different roofs. As we seek to create or sustain a healthy home life, it's important to take a good, long look at those inherited rhythms and decide for ourselves which need to stay and which need to go. In order to fill our lives with the rhythms we value most, we first need to make room for them by clearing out the ruts that keep pulling us off track.

An important part of any healthy family vision will include taking the time to evaluate the rhythms we each bring to the table from our own family of origin. Whether we realize it or not, habits from our childhood have a way of showing up when we least expect it. We have all experienced hearing our parents' words come out of our mouths as we become parents ourselves. ("Money doesn't grow on trees." "This room is a mess!" "Because I told you so!")

Some of us may have a hard time finding any rhythms at all worth repeating. If our childhood was particularly difficult, it can be tempting to throw away our entire bag of inherited rhythms. Others may have a hard time seeing any of their inherited rhythms as potentially harmful ruts to avoid or as simply not a good fit for their new family. What I have learned is that no matter what family you came from, if you look long enough, you can always find at least a few good rhythms to hold on to with gratitude—and usually at least a rut or two it's time to let go of.

One of the ruts Jenni and I determined needed to be removed was fighting in front of the kids. Let me assure you: This is a rut well worth standing against. When we work to make our marriage a thing of beauty, most parenting issues will take care of themselves. Our silent example to our kids speaks more powerfully than any number of words ever will. Very early on we decided that our priority to our kids is to love each other. Not just pretend to, but actually love each other *well*. Trust me, kids know the difference.

One of the healthy rhythms we learned from my family was speaking life. My mom was always really good at doing this. She believed so much in my brother and me and told us continually that we could become anything we wanted to be. Eventually, I started to believe her. Jenni and I want to actively cultivate this rhythm of speaking life and courage over our kids as well.

We are profoundly shaped by the culture of the home we grow up in, and when we reproduce those rhythms in our family, we reproduce that culture. So start by honestly acknowledging what filled your table—the good, the bad, and the ugly—when you were growing up. Choose what you want to take with you, and leave the rest behind.

As you reflect on your own rhythms inherited from the family you grew up in, write down the rhythms you want to continue and the ruts you want to remove. Be as honest and specific as you can. This is just for you.

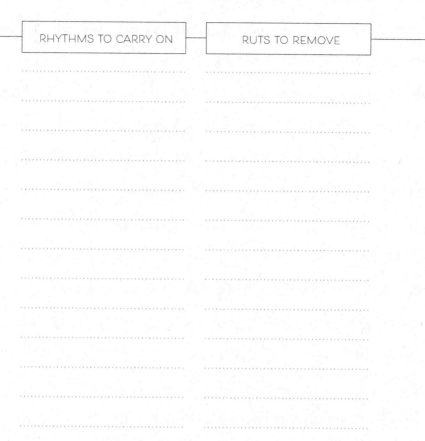

RHYTHMS TO CARRY ON	RUTS TO REMOVE

YOUR ACTUAL FAMILY TABLE

After you've filled in the chart above, involve the kids if you'd like, and discuss how you feel about the current rhythms of your family life. This, of course, is not an opportunity to point fingers. As kindly as you can, make an honest assessment together of the habits of your home.

- Which of our current family rhythms are our favorites?
- Which habits work well in our family?
- Which activities do we find most draining?

- Are there rhythms that need to be removed? Reordered? Repaired?
- What words would others use to describe our family in this season?
- What does our current table look like?

JENNI ————————————————————————————————

Our children are great imitators, so give them something great to imitate.

ANONYMOUS

When one of our daughters was very little, two or three even, she was sitting behind me in her car seat as we pulled to a stop at a traffic light with another car in front of us. Out of her sweet little mouth I heard the words "Go, dude!" I laughed to myself and thought, *Where in the world did she hear that phrase?* That's when I realized: It was from me. I had never even heard myself say those words—until I heard them echoed by my own child. We have undoubtedly all heard words come out of our kids' mouths and wondered the same thing.

If we allow them to, our children can teach us a great deal about who we are becoming and the current state of our own hearts. I love what Mark and Jan Foreman say: "Our children do us a favor: they shine flashlights into our souls."[3] For better or worse, our kids become little mirrors reflecting who we are. Each day, they are literally learning how to live as a human by watching us. Parenting offers a great opportunity to stop and ask, *What are the habits I am passing on to my kids? Do I like the person I am becoming in this season, and if not, how can I change?*

As you reflect on your current table, take a moment to reflect on any "back-seat habits"—alongside any activities you have named that you'd like to keep or remove—that you may be passing on to your kids. Write them down in "Your Current Family Table" that follows. Which ones do you want to continue to develop and cultivate? Which ones will you intentionally let go of? Resist any shame that may arise as you take inventory. There is so much freedom and hope in taking the time to notice and name the truth of where we find ourselves. Only the truth frees us to walk in something more.

Your Current Family Table

SURRENDERING YOUR TABLE

Don't worry about anything; instead, pray about everything.
Tell God what you need, and thank him for all he has done.
Then you will experience God's peace, which exceeds anything
we can understand. His peace will guard your hearts and minds
as you live in Christ Jesus.
PHILIPPIANS 4:6-7, NLT

As we work our way through the core rhythms of thriving families, you might notice that faith is not one of them. You won't find "Jesus" listed as a rhythm all its own. The truth is, He is the underlying foundation of *all* the rhythms. Christ is the source from which all healthy rhythms flow. His strength is what sustains us as we seek to build a thriving family. True change is only available to us through complete dependence on God. The deep, lasting change we long for begins and ends through connecting with God. A flourishing family life is only available by *His* strength. *His* wisdom. *His* guidance. There is no life apart from Him. He is the true Source of all life.

Family psychologist Ross Campbell notes:

> In almost all families that have found contentment, satisfaction, happiness, and genuine thankfulness among all family members, the parents possess a similar priority system. Usually their first priority is of an ethical nature, such as a strong religious faith or moral code. . . . They use this stabilizing relationship to influence all other relationships. . . . Real happiness is found in family orientation—spiritual family, then

physical family. God, spouse, children. These are essential. The remaining priorities are important, of course, but these three must come first.[4]

So our first step toward building our homes is surrendering them to the Lord. We begin by acknowledging that without Him, there's no way we can move toward the family life we long for: "Unless the LORD builds a house, the work of the builders is wasted. Unless the LORD protects a city, guarding it with sentries will do no good" (Psalm 127:1, NLT). We begin to move toward the most beautiful life possible when we surrender to His leading, to His complete partnership in building our life together. I like that word: *partnership*. It reminds me that I'm not alone in this parenting journey. I have a partner to lean on every step of the way.

A life surrendered to God is one where strength flows freely. There's a notable difference between grinding life out in our own strength and discovering the power that becomes available to a heart fully surrendered to Him. As we read in Zechariah 4:6, "'Not by might nor by power, but by my Spirit,' says the LORD." The key to building a strong family is surrendering it to the true Source of life; loosening our grasp for control and letting Him grow the little lives within the walls of our homes as only He can.

Take a moment to pause and spend some time with the Lord. Thank Him for the incredible gift it is to be a family (see Psalm 127:3). For the honor of loving and leading the beloved humans He's entrusted to your care. Surrender the life you are building to His loving hands. And as you look ahead to the life you long to build, ask for His wisdom, truth, and unfailing love to inform each rhythm that fills your home, for His strength to carry you as you practice each one, and for the life that is only available in Him to be the compass continually guiding your family.

On "The Surrendered Table" that follows, list the rhythms, habits, and family priorities you want to surrender to God, trusting that God will grow your family to maturity and flourishing.

The Surrendered Table

PRACTICE

- Name a few families you admire. What sets them apart?

- What healthy rhythms have you noticed in the families you admire?

- Write out a prayer of surrender for your family. Offer up to God the life you are building together, asking Him to lead you, as only He can, to the beautiful life He has for you.

2

WARMTH
WITHIN THE WALLS

The Power of Place

Home is the nicest word there is.

LAURA INGALLS WILDER'S CHARACTER,
***LITTLE HOUSE ON THE PRAIRIE* TV SERIES**

JENNI

Years ago, when Chris and I were pastoring in Texas, we were assigned the task of planting a new church campus in the Dallas–Fort Worth area. Planting the church was one of the greatest joys of our family's life and a sweet season we look back on with great fondness and cherished memories. We loved every single minute of it. I have so many precious pictures of the kids running through the land where the church would be built and sweet family memories of praying for the people who would come. The families we had the honor of pastoring and doing life with in that place became like family to us, and we were marked forever by their friendship and community. Truly such a gift.

One of the tensions of that season, though, was that the church plant landed us in one of the wealthiest suburbs in the city, and on a pastor's salary, with three small kids and a fourth on the way, we couldn't afford much in the area we were in. By God's grace, we found a little brown-brick fixer-upper with great bones and enough bedrooms to house our rapidly growing crew. Over time, and with a lot of hard work, we slowly started to make it feel like home.

Part of the fun of that place was how fixing it up became a community affair. Friends and neighbors helped us build out closets, repair walls, and install hardware. A few sweet friends even came to help me resurface every single kitchen cabinet. We had no idea what we were doing, but we decided to go for it. Sanding, taping, painting, polishing. We may have had to call our husbands a few times to talk us through some steps, but in the end, we nailed it. Thanks to the kindness of community, after only a few short months we were all beginning to feel right at home and so grateful for the sweet space we'd landed in.

Before long, I felt brave enough to host a small-group gathering. The evening was wonderful, from start to finish. It felt so good to finally see our home filled with rhythms that brought us so much life—welcoming people in, pouring steaming-hot cups of coffee, and cozying up for a nice, long night of soul baring by the fire. Tears flowed; hearts poured out. My favorite kind of evening.

As I was reveling in the sweetness of the night, I overheard a casual comment from a new friend about the size of our house.

I knew she wasn't intending to demean or offend, and although I tried to let it roll off my shoulders, the truth is, I couldn't stop thinking about that one remark for the rest of the evening. I let those words surface all kinds of insecurities from deep within me and echo in my mind for weeks. In fact, every time I thought of hosting again after that night, that one comment would always seem to find its way back into my thoughts and tempt me to stop offering up our "tiny little house."

But then the Lord gently began to remind me of all the gatherings over the years that had meant the most to me, and of the experiences that had profoundly changed my life. And I realized the size of the home never mattered at all. In fact, some of my favorite evenings have been spent within the humblest of homes. It was the quality of the company that mattered most— the warmth and friendship and feeling of home they extended toward me. What mattered was the way I felt when I walked through the front door, the welcome I received on the other side, and the love and care created by the ones who lived there. What marked my life were the relationships that had deepened within that home and the meaningful words that were spoken there. What mattered was the warmth within the walls.

NO PLACE LIKE HOME

Home is an important word. What is a home, and what is its purpose? Does our environment even matter? How can we create a place that reflects who we are as a family? A place that extends warmth and welcome to those who enter? How do we intentionally cultivate a space where the rhythms we value most are able to flow freely?

Home is where our life takes place, where the story of our

life together is formed and shaped. Home is a universal longing set deep within us. As poet Maya Angelou said, "The ache
for home lives in all of us, the safe place where we can go as we
are and not be questioned."[1] The home environment we create
becomes a vital piece of the story we tell.

Writer Andi Ashworth notes:

> When handled with care, home enables a person
> or family to move out into the world with deep
> resources to draw upon: a volume of memories where
> close relationships were forged through mealtimes,
> celebrations, special traditions, shared tears and
> laughter, and the reciprocal experience of caring and
> being cared for.[2]

Throughout our years together, we have lived in all different
kinds of homes. By the time we had been married ten years, we
had moved ten times. *Ten.* What I have learned along the way
is that what matters most is not the size or the décor or even
the quality of the home. What matters most is the love and
care felt by the people who enter it, and the dignity, worth, and
welcome they encounter there. That warmth comes from our
gratitude for the place we dwell in and from the ways we exhibit
God's presence in our lives there: creating an environment of
safety and security, establishing regular rituals of belonging, and
developing an atmosphere of goodness.

A beautiful environment of love and warmth can be created
anywhere. There have been several seasons when I struggled to
love the house we lived in, and the temptation for me in those
seasons was to wait. Wait until we lived in a home that felt

more "like us" before I opened it up to others. Wait to cultivate an atmosphere of welcome and warmth until we could find a better space. But over time the Lord showed me that the more I actively searched for things to be grateful for about our home, the more I began to enjoy it. And the more I began to enjoy it, the more free I felt to welcome others in to enjoy it as well.

As Wendell Berry writes in *Hannah Coulter*:

> I think he [the narrator's husband, Nathan] gave up the idea that there is a better place somewhere else. There is no "better place" than this, not in *this* world. And it is by the place we've got, and our love for it and our keeping of it, that this world is joined to Heaven.[3]

SAFE TO CREATE

It is at home where we grow and are nurtured, revitalized, and set on our course to move confidently into the world.

CARRIE GRESS AND NOELLE MERING

On the advice of a trusted writer friend, I bought a pretty leather journal to keep all the thoughts, stories, quotes, and such for this book safely stored in one special spot. It's beautiful. Rich forest green, leather bound, soft pages, with a grosgrain ribbon to mark the spot.

But something strange keeps happening. Each time I sit down to write, I find myself reaching right past the pretty leather journal to grab my spiral scratch pad instead. Somehow, the words just seem to flow more freely in this imperfect, casual notebook than in my beautiful, fancy journal. It's almost like it's giving me permission to just share and write, openly and freely—zero pressure for perfection. Editing can happen later. Here, I am free to just go for it, get it all out, share every thought. Removed from my self-imposed sense that I need to make my words measure up to a beautiful exterior, my casual notebook becomes a safe place.

We want to create the same environment for our kids. We want them to feel the freedom and safety and permission to let it all out, *right here*. To be completely themselves—zero pressure for perfection. This is a safe space. We want to create a home where our kids can grow into the people God's called them to be, where they know they belong, even as they make mistakes along the way.

Cultivating home as a safe space means guiding and leading as needed, but it also means creating a place where our kids are encouraged to really live all the way. Where all their guards can come down. If our home environment is too precious or per-fect, if the purpose of our home shifts from blessing to impress-ing, our kids will begin to look elsewhere for a place where they feel permission to relax and be themselves.

What is the environment we're seeking to create? Is it a place of warmth, where mistakes and real life are welcome? Or are we striving to maintain a level of Pinterest perfection that's simply not possible, increasing our frustration—as well as our family's—by the minute?

There's a notable difference between taking good care of our homes and striving to impress with our homes. You can feel the difference in the air. We've all walked into those homes where the goal is clearly to impress. Everyone feels nervous, fearful of making a mistake at any moment that will disrupt the high level of perfection around them. The opposite is true, as well. We've hopefully all experienced walking through the door of a home where the goal is to welcome and bless. There is something special about the way the home is cared for and the atmosphere that's been cultivated. The intent speaks.

We want our home environment to be one where creativity and discovery are freely encouraged. A lot of times that will mean embracing the mess. This is not easy for me. I like order, beauty, and clean surfaces. My daughters love to rearrange the furniture and make all manner of inventions. I've had to make peace with the mess. Of course, our kids should always be involved in the cleanup, but the point is, we want home to be the place they feel free to try new things and flesh out their many ideas. They can't do that if home is too precious a place to disrupt.

I remember one summer, a particular kid of ours wanted to make a drink machine out of some cardboard boxes and plastic straws they had found in the garage. When they asked me, I'll be honest, my first thought was, *I mean . . . we already have a drinking fountain. It's right there behind you on the front of the fridge; it works perfectly and won't require any energy to clean up afterward.* But then I remembered the kind of confidence I was praying my kids would develop as they grew within our home. I realized this is how it happens: by saying yes to their dreams and ideas. This is right where it happens. So I said yes. And they went to work, building their very own drink dispenser.

When they were finished, they brought us all in to see the final product. And it was . . . a drink dispenser made out of cardboard and straws. But it worked! And they were so proud of it. The look of confidence on their face as they poured out each drink was, of course, what mattered most. Each yes matters.

We want to create a home environment where our kids feel

safe to make mistakes, to struggle and grow, and to try out new dreams and ideas. To succeed and to fail. This is how they become the strong, beautiful people God created them to be. We want to create a home with a foundation that's strong and free enough to support the life within it. We want to create a rich environment where growth and flourishing are possible.

SAFE TO SHARE
CHRIS ──

Ever since our kids were little, they've come home each day brimming with stories to tell. We want our kids to know that when they walk through that door, there is always someone there who will listen. Becoming a safe person to talk things through with can create a safe environment for our kids to share with us. Can we listen without reacting right away? Show empathy for their feelings before correcting?

We want to create rhythms in our home that encourage honest conversation. Bringing in a warm cup of tea and a listening ear at bedtime has opened up countless conversations over the years. For some kids, it's heading out for a walk or a drive. The regular routine of simply making ourselves available to listen when the opportunity arises is the key.

We have found that especially during the teen years, the moments when kids want to talk usually come when you least expect them. You can't force it; you can only embrace it. Just recently, we were cheering for my son at his last baseball game of the season. It was the playoffs, which meant win or go home. The entire school showed up to cheer on the team, and our family was filling the stands, ready for the big win. The atmosphere was electric. We had clobbered this team twice before, so we all thought this would be an easy win and then we'd go on to state. No one can really pinpoint why or how it happened, but it ended up being the worst game the team had experienced all year. The final score was 19–0.

Toward the end of the game, my mother-in-law elbowed me and said, "Hey, Kaden is asking for you." I looked up to catch his eye as he leaned against the fence, warming up to bat next. I jumped up from my seat and headed toward him, hopeful I could say something encouraging in that moment. This was a big loss, and in his seventeen-year-old heart, it felt like the world was crashing down. "Hey, listen to me," I said. "You've done everything you can. You've played a great game. You can hold your head up high. Your team needs you right now. Get out there and get a hit."

He didn't say a word; he just stared out into the field as I spoke. When I finished, the umpire yelled "Play ball!" and it was Kaden's turn to take the plate. Just before he stepped into the batter's box, he looked back at me with a face that said, *Thanks, Dad. I really needed to hear that.* At least, that's the way I took it. The pitcher leaned back and hurled a fastball Kaden's way. With the swing of his bat, Kaden crushed a double into right field. It was the only hit of the night for the team.

In a moment of great pain, my son's eyes had scanned the crowd, searching for mine. I mean, what more could a dad ask for? I'm thoroughly convinced this moment was only possible because of the time Jenni and I have put in with him at home. The late-night talks when my eyes could barely stay open, the listening ear offered as we threw a baseball in the backyard, saying yes to "Hey, Dad, you got a minute?" Each yes created an atmosphere where sharing was valued. Each yes mattered.

RITUALS OF BELONGING

It is hard to say what it means to be at work and thinking of a person you loved and love still who did that same work before you and who taught you to do it. It is a comfort ever and always, like hearing the rhyme come when you are singing a song.

WENDELL BERRY

When you were a kid, what things did your family do that you loved most? Which rituals made you feel most at home? What small moments did you share with your family that stand out to you? Is there a habit you continue in your adult life that carries with it the memory of the one who taught it to you?

Whether you washed the car every weekend with your dad or baked chocolate-chip cookies on Saturdays with your mom, the most ordinary task can become a ritual of belonging when we invite our children to join us in a special way. The seemingly small, ordinary rhythms that keep a home running can serve as great opportunities to instill a sense of worth and belonging in our kids.

Jenni created a rhythm a few mornings a week: After the big kids head out the door to school, she and our little girls grab blankets and books and curl up by the fire to read together. The girls take turns lying in Jenni's lap, coloring and reading, learning and talking. Several times now, our seven-year-old, Kennedi, has leaned in closer to Jenni and said, "I love this, Mom." Years from now when they hear the crackling of logs in the fireplace or catch the scent of burning pine, the hope is it will remind them of home.

A few years ago, I started affirming the girls when they came down the stairs in the morning. "I have something to tell you,"

I always start. "You're smart, you're beautiful, and I love you."
I've done it so often now that they know it's coming. All I have
to say is, "Hey, I have something to tell you," and they can
finish my sentence for me: "Daaaad, I know! I'm smart, I'm
beautiful, and you love me!" It's become a regular rhythm in
our home, one I hope they remember always.

Someday when they grab my arm before I walk them down the aisle, I'll get to say to each one: "I have something to tell you." And they will already know the words that will follow.

The little weekly ways we chase after joy and meaning together help shape our kids' souls.

Saturday morning pancakes. Hikes around Radnor Lake. Family trampoline time and roasting marshmallows around the firepit. Sharing highs and lows around the table at dinnertime. Nature walks down to the creek by our house, collecting leaves and making wishes. The little weekly ways we chase after joy and meaning together help shape our kids' souls. Time spent together is never wasted. And when those little joys become rituals that continue over the years, they begin to create a sense of belonging for our kids. The details of the activities don't even really matter as much as the consistency. Find something you love to do together, and make a regular rhythm out of it.

FILL YOUR HOME WITH GOOD PEOPLE

JENNI ───────────────────────────────

A few months ago, I was praying over a difficult season one of our kids was walking through. What began to stir in my spirit in response from the Lord was this: *Fill your home with good people.*

Sometimes we forget the power we possess to influence our children within the walls of our own home. When they walk out of our front door each day, they are inundated with all sorts of influences we do not get to choose. Teachers, coaches, friends, media—so many people and pressures that will all contribute to the identities of our children. It's just part of life. Some influences will be positive and strengthening. Others will undoubtedly be negative and discouraging. There is so much outside our control.

What we can control, however, is our own home. We can keep a regular stream of interesting, positive influences cycling through our front door. By opening up our home and living in rich community, we get to not only enjoy the company of wonderful people but also teach our kids all manner of valuable life lessons. As they experience the beauty of welcoming others in, they learn what it looks like to care for others, how to make people feel welcome, and what a sweet gift it is to simply delight in being present with others. In an increasingly digital world, with statistics of isolation and loneliness growing by the day, we can choose to fight against the current. We can create an atmosphere of goodness as we fill our homes with good people.

This is a rhythm my parents practiced well when I was growing up. Hospitality was their superpower. Our home was always filled with wonderful humans living interesting, inspiring, quirky, brave, and beautiful lives right in front of us, and we got to watch and learn from them. I was *profoundly* shaped simply by their presence in my life. I got to rub shoulders with their courage, listen in on lessons they learned from mistakes along the way, and receive words of life they took the time to speak over me as a young, impressionable kid. I am so grateful my parents chose to see our home not only as a place to retreat, rest, and recharge but also as a place to regularly welcome others in. As Andi Ashworth writes:

> The home *is* a legitimate and necessary place for us to pull back from the public world, to be quiet, and to find rest and renewal in order to have the inner reserves for giving again. But if that's all it ever is, we'll miss the rich fullness of the life God intends for us.[4]

Fill your home with good people. Bring them around your table. Ask the deep questions, and let your children listen in on the rich responses. It's amazing how my children's ears can miraculously open to hear something I've been trying to tell them for months, simply because it comes out of someone else's mouth. I don't mind. I do the same for my friends' kids. We need each other. Lovingly lean into the lives of the people you care about, speak life into their kids, and invite them to do the same for yours. It's one of the greatest weapons we have against the discouragement of the world around us.

FILL YOUR HOME WITH BEAUTY

We also want to expose our kids to all sorts of wonderful things this world has to offer: baseball and ballet, juicy pomegranates and Texas queso. The sound of Penny & Sparrow, the scent of fresh roses, and the sight of the sun setting over the water. We want to let them taste and see all that's good and beautiful in the world around us and create in them what Jan Foreman calls an "appetite for the good":

Rather than letting pop culture and shallow culture give our kids an appetite for "sugary things," we can create in them a depth and an appreciation for what's really good, true, and beautiful.[5]

Instead of making them fear the world or letting them settle for a cheap imitation of the good, we can give our kids an appreciation for what's truly beautiful in the world by filling our home and life with a taste of those marvelous things. Start with what you love. What are the things that bring you delight or stir your soul? Make a special place for them in your home and in your family life. Introduce your kids to your favorite James Taylor record, invite them into the kitchen to help bake your grandmother's famous blackberry cobbler, or slice open a juicy, ripe Bartlett pear together. Share with them the beauty that you know.

I love how author John Eldredge notes, "Beauty brings hope, and beauty reassures you of the goodness of God."[6] Incorporating regular touchpoints of the beauty available to us in the world God has given us brings life and hope to our souls. It lifts our spirits and shifts the environment of our homes more than we realize. Even a simple vase of cut stems from the yard placed on the breakfast table can offer a little light to those who pass by. When we actively look for the beauty around us and share it with our children, we help them develop eyes to see it and hearts to receive it as they grow.

How we live together matters. I can't control what will happen tomorrow, but I can choose to fill my home with the rhythms that bring life to my family today. Home provides the best opportunity to show our kids what we know to be true, good, and beautiful. We share with them the best of what we've learned and what makes us come alive, and we guide them as they seek to find what they love and what brings life to them as well.

DO IT ANYWAY

CHRIS ─────────────────────────────────

A mantra Jenni and I have started saying to each other in this season—with two teenagers, one tweenager, and two little ones—is "Do it anyway."

We cannot control our kids' responses to the rhythms we fill our homes with. In parenting, A + B does not always equal C. Sometimes our kids will respond well immediately, with joy and gratitude, and sometimes they won't. What the Lord has been teaching us over and over in this season is that we are not in charge of their responses. Our job is to be the parents He has called us to be, regardless of our children's reactions. There will be days when we ask ourselves, *Does anything I am doing matter at all?* We can decide in advance to remind ourselves of the truth in these moments. It does matter. It all matters. If we make our choices based on how we think our kids will respond, it can keep us from giving them what they need most: our unconditional, unwavering love and faithfulness.

Ask your kids the deep, meaningful questions. What if they roll their eyes? Do it anyway. Plan the family night. What if the kids complain? Do it anyway. Put the devices away for the afternoon! What if they throw a fit? Do it anyway.

It will all count in the long run. Sometimes they'll thank you for it, and other times they won't. Sometimes they'll energetically participate in your family night, and other times they won't participate at all. Do it anyway. Their reactions to your efforts don't get to dictate the rhythms you fill your home with. You get to choose the habits that make up your home. Seek God for His best rhythms for your family, and then practice them faithfully, trusting Him with the results. There is a harvest coming if you don't give up. Trust the story He is writing. *Do it anyway.*

Ultimately, we want our homes to be the places where our kids know that they are loved and that they belong. I love what beloved children's show host Fred Rogers said:

> The roots of a child's ability to cope and thrive, regardless of circumstance, lie in that child's having had at least a small, safe place (an apartment, a room, a lap) in which, in the companionship of a loving person, that child could discover that he or she was lovable and capable of loving in return. If a child finds this during the first years of life, he or she can grow up to be a competent, healthy person.[7]

There's so much pressure for our kids to perform, to prove their worth, and to constantly measure up. We want to make sure they know there is at least one place where they are always loved, always welcomed, and completely delighted in *just as they are.* It's right here with us. It's called *home.*

PRACTICE

- Share with your family a ritual of belonging that was particularly meaningful to you as a kid.

- What is the warmest home you've ever walked into? What made it feel that way?

- Are there any current family rituals that make you feel at home? Share them with your family.

- Write down a few words you hope others—including those who live there—feel when they enter your home. Brainstorm some ideas to create an environment that lines up with the words you chose.

3

IT TAKES A VILLAGE

Building a Strong Community

As iron sharpens iron,
so one person sharpens another.

PROVERBS 27:17

Growing up, we all probably had those families within our communities who stood out to us, who left a mark on us for the better. Who lived on in our memories and sparked a dream within us of the family of our own we hoped to have someday.

I was ten years old when I met the Adler family. Michael was the new worship pastor at our church that year, and Linda became my voice teacher for the next eight years. Every week, Linda would teach my voice lessons at the black upright piano in the front room of their home while their rowdy boys would wrestle and play down the carpeted hallway. I just loved being in their home. The Adlers were warm and funny and creative, and I don't remember a single voice lesson that didn't end in roaring laughter. They were a family who had *fun* together, who seemed to genuinely enjoy one another. I remember the distinct sense of being deeply cared for whenever I was in their presence. They always dropped whatever they were doing to be fully present with me, to ask questions about my life, about school and boys and faith.

Over the years, the Adlers became close friends with our family and a vital part of the village that raised me. They put in the time to take a profound interest in my life. They were there to cheer me on as I grew in my gifts over the years, trying all manner of things along the way. Some that seemed to fit well, and plenty that did not. They felt free to call me out when I drifted off course from the person they knew God had called me to be.

I remember a specific "talking to" in high school that I received from Michael after singing for church one Sunday in a shirt that was a little on the too-tight side. "Jen, let me tell you something," he said. "When you use the beautiful voice God has given you while dressed immodestly, it's as if you have placed a dancing monkey on your head. No one can even pay attention to the beautiful song you are singing because they are so distracted by the monkey dancing on your head." It's often only in hindsight that we appreciate such wisdom.

There was also an older man in my church who became a vital part of the village that raised me. His name was Mr. Amend. I will never know exactly why, but for some reason, he just decided that I was one of *his*. From the moment I met him at the age of eleven, he decided to care about me and regularly went out of his way to pour into my young life. That man consistently prayed for me over the next fifteen years! And by "prayed for me," I mean that he *wrote out* the prayers he would pray over me, encouraging the giftings he noticed God developing in me, and he took the time to put them in a card and mail them to my house . . . for *fifteen years*. All throughout middle and high school, when I went away to college, and even as I got married and became a mother. I mean, who does that? What a remarkable gift.

He made me feel special and cared for and believed in. He was always on the lookout for opportunities for me to grow in the gifts he saw in me. He led the senior adult ministry at our church, and he would ask me to sing for his class several times throughout the year. As I grew older, he would send opportunities my way as he discovered them. When I was in middle school, he found an advertisement for a local youth theater company and mailed it to me—circled and marked with my name on it. Later, in high school, I got to spend two summers traveling the world with a singing group I had discovered the same way: through a clipped article that arrived in my mailbox from Mr. Amend, circled and starred, with my name on it.

On my wedding day, as I was fluffing my dress and touching up my lip gloss, I heard a knock on the door. My mom had snuck Mr. Amend and his wife into the bridal room to pray over me just before I walked down the aisle. I mean, what a remarkable gift. His words, his care, his unwavering belief in me over the years were among the greatest gifts of my young life—far greater than he probably ever knew. I hope I said it a million times while you were here with us, Mr. Amend, but just in case I didn't say it enough: "Thank you. . . . I am a life that was changed."[1]

These are the kinds of remarkable humans I pray God will send across my children's paths as they grow. They are people who seem to take seriously the instruction from St. Paul to "be devoted to one another in love. Honor one another above yourselves" (Romans 12:10). The truth is, we don't raise our kids alone. We carry with us the voices, support, and influence of the relationships around us. If there's anything I've learned as a parent, it's that I *can't* do this alone. It takes a village, a strong village, to raise strong kids. We can be intentional with the kind of village we're creating as we raise our children. The people we trust to speak into our children's lives become significant parts of their stories.

The village we create begins, of course, with us as their parents, and it moves beyond us to include extended family and friends who become like family to us.

Several of our girls love to craft. Neither of their parents is very good at it. But Chris's mom is the queen of crafting. Anytime she comes for a visit, we know she will arrive carrying crates of projects to make with our girls, and we are so grateful. She is so good at listening to their creative ideas, taking them seriously, and coaching them to bring their projects to life. She and our kids enter into a completely different world together as they get lost in bringing a dream to life. She has made Texas Rangers pillows with our son, paintings and purses and elaborate cardboard houses with our girls. They have learned a lot from her and have been shaped profoundly by her encouragement and enthusiasm for their ideas over the years.

Take a moment to look across the landscape of the unique community God has placed you in. Ask Him to bring to mind the relationships worth leaning into and cultivating as you build your family's village. Members of your extended family, neighbors, friends from church, really anyone who is relationally healthy and aligned with your values—look for ways to involve them in your family's village.

Ask God to bring the Mr. Amends and the Adlers into your world, and find opportunities to show that kind of extraordinary care to those around you as well. Are there families in your community you could begin to encourage and pour into? Start by praying for them, and ask God to show you specific ways you could come alongside them as they grow.

CHRIS ——————————————————————————————

You are the average of your top five friends.[2] I never liked that saying. Initially, it made me want to fight back, feeling it couldn't possibly be true. But the more I've chewed on it over the years, the more I've realized that it does feel pretty accurate. We tend to land somewhere in the middle of those we spend most of our time with. Whether we like it or not, we are all greatly influenced by the people around us.

True friendship is one of life's richest blessings . . . and a vital part of raising and cultivating a healthy family. God has wired us to thrive when we care for others and allow ourselves to be cared for by them. Irish philosopher and poet John O'Donohue noted, "Our friends are the mirrors where we recognize ourselves, and quite often it is their generosity of spirit that has enabled us to grow and flourish."[3]

But it's important to make sure that our closest friends, the ones we surround ourselves with most, are pointing us in the right direction. If I am trying to practice healthy rhythms in my family, for example, and create a culture that's wholesome and encouraging and life-giving, but I am surrounding myself with relationships that are moving in the opposite direction of those rhythms, it will be very hard for me to get where I want to go.

The journey of parenting will lead us through all different kinds of days. We will need strong, true friends around us to lean on through the deepest valleys as well as to celebrate with on the joyous mountaintops. I can't tell you how many times God has shown up for us in our darkest hours through the friendships around us and used us to be there for others on their toughest days. It's the great gift of community. Philosopher Albert Schweitzer noted, "Often, too, our own light goes out, and is rekindled by some experience we go through with a fellow man. Thus we have each of us cause to think with deep gratitude of those who have lighted the flames within us."[4]

Take a deeper look at your closest friendships. Do those relationships spur you on and strengthen you as you attempt to build a flourishing family? Do they bring out the best in you and keep pointing you to what is true? Take an inventory of the advice you receive from your inner circle. Is it advice you would give to your own children? Do you have at least a handful of friends who seem to enjoy their children and view them as a gift to treasure, or are they constantly complaining about the children they've been entrusted with?

As poet William Blake said, we become what we behold.[5] A few important questions to consider when evaluating our closest friendships: *Do I want what they have? Do they have a family life that inspires me? A marriage I hope to learn from in some way?*

If the answers are no, begin praying for the Lord to surround you with healthy, loving, safe people. They're out there. Seek them out, invite them into your home, and pour time into cultivating those friendships.

A COMMUNITY OF HONOR

Whoever guards his mouth and tongue
Keeps his soul from troubles.
PROVERBS 21:23, NKJV

As we work to build a strong community, we want to make sure we're honoring our children and the remarkable people they're becoming along the way. As we grow closer to others, it can be very tempting to divulge the details of our latest parenting struggle to whomever will listen. Connecting with friends over a shared parenting struggle can feel like bonding. But the truth is, there's a big difference between processing openly with close, trusted people and carelessly complaining about our kids to anyone who will listen. One is for healing; the other is for venting. One seeks health; the other poisons.

Complaining about our kids' behavior or faults is not helpful to our kids or to us, and the truth is, the details of their personal struggles are simply not ours to share. What I have learned from the experience of falling into this trap is that, at the heart of it, it's usually an attempt to feel less alone in the struggle parenting can be at times. But when I remember the truth that I'm never alone in any season I am walking through with my child—when I remember I have partnered with the Lord to raise these precious gifts He's given me—then I no longer feel the need to connect with others in that way. It might feel good in the moment, but it never lasts long; regret inevitably follows.

We are all a work in progress—all of us. We all have things we're doing well and things we're struggling with. We are wise to keep the best of who our kids are becoming always in our hearts and minds, and to speak of them with the dignity and worth they deserve, even when talking through their struggles with our trusted friends. Look for the good and make much of it. Share with others in your village the ways you see your kids trying and growing and persevering. There's always something good to find. Pray for eyes to see it.

A COMMUNITY OF TRUTH

JENNI ───

Let us not become weary in doing good, for at the proper time we will reap a harvest if we do not give up.

GALATIANS 6:9

One of God's favorite ways to speak to us is through His people. It's so important to have a handful of friends in our family village who will speak the truth over us when we need it most.

A few months ago, as Chris and I were deep in the throes of writing this book, the Lord sent us the sweetest gift through one of our village friends, Christy.

When we moved back to Franklin almost five years ago, Christy was one of the very first friendships God brought into my life. In that season, being the new girl in town, I was so thankful to find a deep soul who was ready and willing to cut past the chitchat and dive right into the good stuff: matters of the heart. Over the years, she has become like a big sister to me, encouraging me in faith and life and motherhood, praying over me in crucial moments, and just offering a listening ear and a warm cup of coffee on the days when I need it most.

While Chris and I have been working on this book, Christy and her husband, Nate, have been working on a project of their own: her latest record. We have encouraged and prayed over each other and checked in on progress along the way. A few months ago, she sent me the final, finished product, and it just happened to be on one of those hard days when I needed a fresh reminder of God's promises. As I hit play and took in each song, the tears began to flow. Over and over, God met me through the melodies. I could not believe how right on time each word was as I listened.

One of the songs quickly became a theme song for this book and an encouragement for the tumultuous task parenting can often be:

> *So keep on shining and doing good,*
> *Even when it's the hardest thing you've done.*
> *Even when no one's looking,*
> *There's a promise if you don't give up.*[6]

It's hard, good work, this parenting thing. Sometimes it feels like the hardest thing you've ever done. Sometimes it feels like no one sees all the work you're putting in. There are certain seasons along the way when we ask ourselves, *Does this work I'm doing even matter?* We need close friends who can encourage us through all types of days. These words from our village friend were such a sweet reminder of the promise that carries us. There is a good harvest growing, underneath the surface, in each season. And this is the promise: We will reap that harvest if we don't give up.

There is no such thing as a perfect family. There will be plenty of bumps and bruises along the way. Even the healthiest parents on the planet have extremely hard days and veer off track. That's just part of life. The important thing is that we get back up and keep on going. Keep doing the hard but good work of loving. Keep speaking words of life, keep showing up for each other, keep choosing gratitude. Lean on the incredible village around you, and trust the story God is writing. Trust His hand to take you where only He can. Keep on.

PRACTICE

- Who were some of the members of the village who raised you?

- When you were growing up, which families sparked hope in your heart for your future family?

- What aspects of these families stood out to you?

- Which people in your current community are a key part of your family's village?

- Reflect on your unique community. Are there any new relationships worth investing in that come to mind? Invite them over for dinner this month.

- Ask your kids which friends in their lives mean the most to them. Get to know their top five friends.

PART TWO

THE CORE
RHYTHMS

IN THIS SECTION, we'll dive into the five core rhythms that have become lifelines to us over the last eighteen years of family life. They are intentional rhythms learned from flourishing families that have gone before us—who have taken the time to pour into our lives over the years. Practices learned through pausing and paying attention to the deepest convictions of our hearts. We did not invent these rhythms on our own, nor did the families who passed them on to us. As it turns out, they are straight from God's Word. Jesus was the ultimate example of how to love others well—including the little ones who live within our homes.

We pray that as you dive into these rhythms, they will become like a good song you won't be able to get out of your head, and that as you begin to practice them, you will discover new levels of connection, closeness, and flourishing in your family's life. As you discover each new rhythm, pause and take a deeper look at the season God has placed you in. We hope the unique blessings of your specific family and these sweet days you have together will be illuminated in new ways before your eyes. We pray that as only He can, God will open your eyes to see the remarkable gifts He has for you in this very season, ready to be opened and enjoyed.

4

GRACE IS THE WORD

The Rhythm of Speaking Life

Shower the people you love with love,
Show them the way that you feel.
Things are gonna work out fine,
If you only will.
JAMES TAYLOR

JENNI

Having a baseball-playing big brother has meant that our four girls have spent quite a lot of time at baseball fields. Cheering on the team usually loses its luster after about ten minutes, and eventually they venture out to find their own more exciting games to play. This has led to all manner of creative activities. Building red-dirt forts for their dolls, seeing who can climb the surrounding trees the highest, and choreographing dances to perform for the audience, who surely must need something else to watch besides the boring baseball game.

One of their favorite pastimes has been finding a nearby vacant field where they could race each other around the plates. "Take a video, Mom!" our six-year-old pleaded before one particular race. She took her place at the starting line next to her four-year-old sister, looked at me with a twinkle in her eye, and shouted, "On your mark, get set, go!" They took off as fast as their little legs could carry them. Pretty quickly, our six-year-old's longer legs gave her an advantage over her younger sister. As big sis Kensi took the lead, I leaned in to see what little Keris would do. I watched in surprise as Keris's smile got bigger and bigger the farther and farther Kensi got in front of her. Though her little arms kept pumping and her tiny legs kept running, I heard her call out in her sweet little voice, "Go, Kensi, go! Go, Kensi, go!" My heart melted. She was cheering on the one who was beating her, seemingly unaware that they were even racing at all.

Her goal was not to beat her big sister—it was simply to enjoy the race. And when she caught sight of someone she loved doing well, even when success meant being passed up, she instinctively cheered her on with all her might. She found joy in running her own race, not in competing with anyone else. And the sound of her little voice cheering for her sister with so much joy has stayed with me. How I hope to live like Keris. And oh, how I hope my girls will always cheer each other on like that. No matter what season they find themselves in. I hope they will speak life to one another, giving each other the gift of becoming one another's biggest cheerleaders in the great race of life.

Think for a moment of the families you've admired most throughout your life. The siblings who've maintained the strongest bonds over the years. The family that seems to love, care for, and genuinely enjoy one another. If you were to pull back the curtain on their family life and look at how they speak to and about each other, I guarantee you would see this rhythm of speaking life as an integral part of their home. Thriving families choose to speak words of life.

The other day, my mom sent me this quote she found in an antique shop: "There are many things in life that will catch your eye, but only a few will catch your heart. Pursue those."[1] Throughout the years, whenever I encounter this practice of speaking life, it never ceases to catch my heart. It always feels remarkable. In a world that can be so full of hate, so full of competition, cattiness, and criticism, hearing a kind word spoken feels like discovering a diamond in the rough.

Our words matter. As Proverbs 18:21 (NKJV) tells us, "Death and life are in the power of the tongue." The words we speak over one another have the potential to build life in us or to destroy us. We have been given incredible power to build up those we love or to tear them down, simply through the words that come out of our mouths. The truth is, we create the culture of our homes by the words we choose to speak. If we want to create a thriving family, we must begin by considering our words.

> Thriving families choose to speak words of life.

Parents we admire most have this remarkable way of speaking about their children with a great sense of dignity, respect, and admiration. They hold each other up like trophies, in the best way possible. Through all the highs and lows, they find a way to cling to the best version of each member of their family and choose to speak to that person. Each day we have a choice: We can look for all the faults to correct in our children, or we can search for the good and speak it out loud.

There's a recognizable element of grace in the words spoken within a healthy family culture. Grace looks like holding our tongue when we're tempted to criticize. Grace chooses to highlight the best we see in each other rather than focus on each other's faults. Grace gives us the ability to laugh over the spilled glass of milk rather than explode with anger and frustration. Grace reminds us we are all on a journey of growth and we all make mistakes.

What an incredible gift we've been given, one that requires careful stewardship! Every word spoken over children throughout their lifetimes will affect them in some way, but our words—as their parents, the most powerful influence in their lives—carry the most weight. All the more reason to proceed with great caution when speaking over these impressionable little gifts we've been given. John O'Donohue noted, "We have no idea the effect we actually have on one another. This is where blessing can achieve so much. Blessing as powerful and positive intention can transform situations and people."[2] One of the most powerful ways we can bless our kids and point them toward becoming who they are called to be is by intentionally speaking words of life on a regular basis.

UNNECESSARY CRITICISM

The other night, Chris and I were reading a bedtime story to our girls, taking our turn on each page. Usually, we tag team the bedtime process. With five rambunctious kids and only two parents, this teamwork is simply a logistical necessity. You take a few, I take a few. Efficiency wins. But on this particular evening, our older ones happened to be spending the night with friends, so we found ourselves with a little extra margin and got to enjoy the bedtime routine together, with just our two youngest girls.

As we read each page, I noticed something. When Chris missed a word or accidentally misread something, I didn't correct him at all. It didn't matter. That wasn't the point. The point was the moment we were enjoying with our daughters and the delight we got to experience together. I was thinking how grateful I am to have a husband who is such a great dad to our girls—who stops what he's doing to join in the bedtime routine, scooping them up into his lap to read them a story. I knew it was the end of a long work week for Chris and how tired he must have felt, but he chose them anyway, and I was so grateful. There's no way in the world I would have tainted the moment by focusing on a missed word in the story. I respect him too much, and I care too much about the way my girls see him. I want them to be grateful for that moment as well—grateful they have a dad who will read them a story, not because he's a flawless reader but because he's an amazing dad.

Something about that moment stayed with me, and I couldn't stop thinking about it. It was so easy for me to stop myself when the temptation to critique Chris arose. I thought of the respect I have toward Chris that comes so easily—and in contrast, how hard it is for me to show that same respect toward my kids at times. I thought of the tension I'd experienced earlier in the week with one of my teenagers. I thought of how often I had jumped at the chance to correct each mistake. I'm their mom, after all. If I don't point these things out, how will they learn and grow and change? Isn't that my job?

But as the Lord kept gently guiding my thoughts, I remembered that my job isn't to change them. That's not the point.

The point is the relationship we are building together and the love I extend toward them. *Maybe this teen thing would go a lot smoother*, I thought, *if I stopped focusing on correcting them and just loved them as they are, remembering I am a work in progress too. If I worked to actively look for things to be grateful for about who they are and speak those things over them. If I asked the Lord to show me where He is growing and changing them and how I can celebrate those things.*

> Love prospers when a fault is forgiven.
>
> PROVERBS 17:9, NLT

So much of parenting can start to feel centered on constant correction. After all, it's a loving thing to correct when needed. We all need instruction at times. It's easy to fall into the habit, though, of constantly finding fault; of overlooking all the good things our children are doing as well. If all they ever hear from us is what they're doing wrong, it can begin to cause a great deal of damage to their hearts and to our relationship.

The truth is, we cannot change unless we feel loved and accepted at a foundational level. The Lord is patiently showing me that when I focus on finding the good, I begin to see it everywhere. There is always something good we can notice and name about our kids, even if it's as small as pointing out when they say thank you.

I'm also learning that there is no need to express every single wrong that I notice. Is it imperative to their growth that I point it out? Or is it something I can let go of? It is the kindness of the Lord that leads us to repentance (Romans 2:4). His kindness, not His criticism, leads us to repentance. Our goal is always reconciliation. The goal is always to grow the relationship, to get to the hearts of our children, not to prove ourselves right.

When we intentionally speak life over our family, rewards tend to appear. Here are a few thought starters on how to practice this rhythm in your home.

SPEAK TO THE GOOD

Creating the rhythm of speaking life in your family culture has a simple starting point: When you think something nice, say it out loud. Affirm the developing character you see in your child or the kindness you observe them display. Take their sweet face in your hands and tell them something you love about how God made them. Speak to them with respect and honor, as someone worthy of love and dignity. Look for ongoing opportunities to encourage your kids. When you think something nice, say it out loud.

Work on treating yourself that way as well. As we begin to see ourselves as loved and delighted in by the Lord, treating our kids that way will flow almost effortlessly.

Our kids will have billions of words spoken over them throughout their lifetimes. We want our kids to be able to discern what is true. The greatest way we can teach them this skill is by speaking words of truth over them. Let them learn what truth sounds like. Becoming familiar with truth will empower our kids to recognize a lie when they hear it. Take

> Becoming familiar with truth will empower our kids to recognize a lie when they hear it.

every moment you can to encourage your kids. The simple act of speaking a kind word can do wonders for the love we long to communicate to our kids and the relationship we're building between us.

This rhythm has been transformative for our family. Daily words of care communicate love to our kids and deepen the relationship we're growing. That practice can be spontaneous; it can also be planned. Here are some ideas of regular practices that can help bring this rhythm to life.

Bedtime Blessings

Take a moment every night at bedtime to share an encouragement based on something you noticed in your child during the day. Maybe it's the card they made for their big sister because she had a hard day. Maybe it was the toy he decided to share, or the B+ she got on that stressful spelling test. Look for the good you see growing in them, and then nurture it by taking a moment to name it out loud, affirming it in them.

Birthday Blessings

Another practice we've found helpful in cultivating this habit of speaking to the good in our home is taking a moment on each family member's birthday to speak a blessing over them. As we're enjoying their favorite meal, we each take a turn to say something we love and are grateful for about that person. It's become a favorite family tradition, and our kids are now the ones to remind us if we forget it!

This is definitely a practice our kids have grown into as the years go by. When they're younger, the birthday blessings they speak might be small and simple, but as they grow and mature, sometimes they will surprise you with a deep, meaningful birthday blessing. Because it's become a regular rhythm, they know it's coming and have time to prepare. This past year, at seventeen, our son delivered a birthday blessing for Chris that had us both in tears! Let them grow into this practice over time.

Childhood Journals

Keep a blessing journal for each child. So much of our work as adults involves returning to the beauty, innocence, goodness, and gifting we lived in so effortlessly as children. As John O'Donohue wrote, "The beginning often holds the clue to everything that follows."[3] As an adult, I have often wished I had a journal of my childhood, chronicling the things I loved, the things that came naturally to me, and the fingerprints of God throughout my early years.

So I keep a journal for each of our kids in my nightstand to write down different things I see in them as they grow. I record important events and character traits that seem important to who they're becoming. And at every birthday I write them a letter in their journal to affirm the things I see God is growing in them in that season. Struggles they're overcoming, gifts and talents and strengths I see developing in them. I write to them as the adults I hope they'll become.

I love to journal, so this practice comes naturally to me, but if there's another way you like to express the good things you see growing in your kids, go for it! Chris likes to keep a running voice memo on his phone of positive things he's noticing in each kid.

Praise before Presents

Similar to birthday blessings, another tradition we've started on Christmas morning, before we open presents, is to take turns sharing out loud what we are most grateful for about each family member. I want my kids to remember that our words of love and honor are the greatest gifts we can give each other. It's a tradition I hope they all carry with them!

SPEAK TO THE GIFTING

Growing up, my dad struggled in school. He later became a brilliant architect and a successful businessman, but as a kid, his undiagnosed dyslexia left him feeling downright dumb a lot of the time in classes where he just couldn't keep up. One afternoon during his senior year, an art teacher took him aside after class and said, "You know, Steve, you're *really* good at drawing. The way you're able to see in 3-D as you sketch is a great skill I see in you. Have you ever thought of becoming an architect?"

Those simple words of kindness changed the course of my dad's life. Suddenly, a brand-new door opened before him. That teacher took the time to speak a blessing over him and point to a gifting she saw in him, and as she did, she helped put him on the pathway to an important calling on his life.

I love how John O'Donohue put it:

The beauty of blessing is its belief that it can affect what unfolds. . . . A blessing awakens future wholeness. We use the word *foreshadow* for the imperfect representation of something that is yet to come. We could say that a blessing "forebrightens" the way. When a blessing is invoked, a window opens in eternal time.[4]

Part of any thriving family culture is the habit of looking for and affirming the gifts, talents, and callings we see developing in our kids. The rhythm of speaking life reaches a new level when we make it a priority to notice and name our kids' natural strengths. The childhood experience of hearing a positive word that becomes a clue to a calling or ability is something we never forget. Encourage your kids in the gifts they've been given, and look for ways they can contribute those skills to your family and community.

SPEAK TO THE POTENTIAL

When I was a young college student in my early twenties, one of my favorite families from my childhood years served as a home away from home. They lived just a few hours from where I went to school, so when I found myself craving the comforts of family or a home-cooked meal, I would drive down to see them for the weekend. (Sidenote: If you happen to have college students in your community, especially those far from home, one of the best ways you can bless them is by inviting them over for a home-cooked meal. It is highly likely they are eating a steady diet of cereal and soda. Show them a little pot roast love.)

On one such visit, I experienced an early lightbulb moment about what it means to create a thriving family. The evening was winding down after a lovely meal together with the family and several friends from the community, including Susan, a single woman in her thirties. We were enjoying the end of the evening, and one by one, the local guests started to head home. A while later, the father, Michael, called out to his eleven-year-old son: "Hey bud, would you call Miss Susan and make sure she made it home okay?" I looked back at the eleven-year-old, ready for the protest I assumed would come. He was only eleven, after all, and this seemed like a very adult task. "Sure, Dad!" he said, and headed toward the phone.

I have never forgotten that moment. Deep down, I made a mental note: *Wise parents expect great things from their kids*. They keep in mind the kind of adult they hope their kids will some-day become, and they speak to them accordingly. They offer their kids opportunities to grow in character.

Wise parents expect great things from their kids.

The truth is, in that moment, the character qualities of love and thoughtfulness belonged to Michael, and he could have easily made the phone call himself. Instead, he saw an opportunity to pass his values of thoughtfulness and love on to his son, giving *him* the opportunity to become the kind of person who thinks of and shows care for others.

For better or worse, our kids will rise or fall to meet the expectations we communicate to them through our words. It's important to keep in mind who our children are becoming, rather than defining them by how they are acting in a specific season. I know from experience that this is easier said than done. We can ask the Lord to give us His eyes to see our children as He does, then speak words of life to the person *He* sees. Let's look for opportunities to call our children higher.

THINK TRAINING

Sometimes developing the potential in our children requires withholding the answers they're asking for so that they have the space they need to find them on their own. Searching for answers to our own questions is how we grow.

There was a running joke in the religion department at Belmont University, where I spent most of my early twenties, that the professors would never answer a question directly. They were famous for it. They would only ever respond to a question with a question. As a student, I found this maddening, as did many of my peers. But as an adult, I can see what a valuable gift our professors were giving us. They were training us to think on our own. Up until that point, we had relied on our parents or teachers or coaches for all the answers. The time had come to learn to think for ourselves. The faculty were forming in us a new habit: seeking the answers we needed without consulting others for every question we encountered.

We want to teach our kids to learn how to think on their own. Instead of handing them every answer, what if we coached them to search for answers on their own? The truth is, we can't always be with our children. Many of the decisions they will make will happen when we are not around. We want them to be able to make the best decisions possible based on the truth of what they know to be right and good, not because their parents are watching. "Think training" happens as we listen to our kids' problems, ask them good questions, and allow them to find the right solutions for themselves.

Ultimately, speaking to the potential in our children means

holding on to the people they are, in all their depth and beauty and goodness, and allowing them the space they need to travel down life's road, trying on new things along the way. All the while, as parents, we can serve as a safe harbor, reminding them of the best of who they truly are in every season.

MARK THE MOMENT WITH WORDS
CHRIS

We can all look back and remember words that were spoken over us that left a mark in some way. Words that began to draw something out of us or open a new pathway before us. Words have that power.

One of the most meaningful ways we have found to practice this rhythm of speaking life involves a rite-of-passage party when our kids turn thirteen. At this point, we've had two Graebe kids cross over this threshold. Each night was tailored to the uniqueness of the child, but the main elements remained the same. With the permission of our two eldest kids, we'd love to share some of those elements with you in hopes of sparking ideas for your own family on how to mark this important milestone for your child with words of blessing they can carry with them into their future.

For our daughter's rite-of-passage party, we invited a handful of women in our community who know her well—mentors, leaders, teachers, and friends—to join us for a meal and a time of blessing. These women each spoke a blessing over her, highlighting her beauty, giftings, and potential. We also felt the Lord leading us to invite a few of her peers. We hesitated at first, worrying they wouldn't take it seriously or grasp the power of the moment, but we are so glad we listened to the Lord's leading.

Each friend included a special gift based on the word they chose to speak over her, and we were all so blown away by the blessings they gave. It was a highlight of the night.

Another element that we felt the Lord leading us toward was how important it was for me, her dad, to be involved in the event. According to Jenni's research, these types of events typically include only men for a young man or women for a young woman. But Jenni and I know how vital a dad's relationship with his daughter is, especially during adolescence, and God was nudging us to pay attention to that. So I joined Jenni in planning the party, which was a blessing for us to do together. I helped pull off the surprise by driving Addie to the house where the women were waiting for her. I prayed to open the evening, and then spoke the first blessing.

For our son's rite-of-passage night, it went fairly similarly, but with fewer women and way more meat! The room was filled with coaches, mentors, teachers, and family. I'll never forget seeing Kaden sitting in a chair just in front of our fireplace and listening as man after man who had watched him grow and change over the years shared strengths and gifts and talents they noticed in him. Some spoke to the young man he was in that moment, and others spoke to the man he would someday become. The crowning moment of the night was when his grandfather spoke a powerful blessing over him. Obviously, since the room was full of tough dudes, I can neither confirm nor deny that there wasn't a dry eye in the house. But we all concluded that any tears in our eyes must have been from that dry rub on the brisket.

I don't know what our kids will remember from those nights, but I do know that we poured out every drop of love over them that we possibly could. We gave them the greatest gift we could in that crucial moment of transition: blessing.

I love what John O'Donohue said: "A blessing awakens future wholeness."[5] Just as Jenni's dad was pointed toward future success by his art teacher's words of encouragement, the blessings we speak over our kids point them toward the good plans the Lord has for them. Look for the good, and speak it aloud.

May you and I remember what an incredible gift we've been given: the power to speak life-giving words over our kids. To model each day what it looks like to push competition aside and cheer each other on. As we run this race of family life together, may we remember the weight our words hold and choose each day to practice this rhythm that cultivates a thriving family life.

PRACTICE

- Pray for eyes to see the good in each of your family members and for the courage to speak it out loud.

- Looking for the good and speaking life can be difficult to do, especially if you did not grow up experiencing this practice. Give yourself the grace of starting small. Write a note of prayer or encouragement to someone on a particularly stressful or important day. Offer a simple compliment. Over time, you will notice your capacity start to grow.

- Praise your kids in public this week (in front of actual humans, not on social media). Find something you can genuinely affirm in your kids, and then do it in a sincere way in front of your friends or family. Watch them lift their heads a little higher.

5

MY LIFE FOR YOURS

> Truly I tell you, whatever you did for one of the least
> of these brothers and sisters of mine, you did for me.
> **MATTHEW 25:40**

CHRIS

My brother and I have always been extremely close. We experienced a lot of ups and downs together throughout our childhood, which developed a deep, unbreakable bond between us. When I went off to college, I would often drive back to our hometown to see my brother play under the Friday night lights or zoom around the track for a meet.

One particularly incredible mid-April day, I just couldn't resist the urge to ditch my classes and head to my brother's track meet. There was a slightly cool breeze in the air, the sun was shining, and it was just a perfect day for running. Eric was a sprinter, just like me and our dad. We ran races like the 100- and 200-meter dashes, as well as various relays.

My favorite race was the 4×100 relay, which consisted of a team of four individuals spread equally around the track, each running about 100 meters per leg and then passing the baton to their teammate. In my track days (insert old-man voice here) when I ran this relay, I was typically the lead leg for our team.

On this day, Eric had been selected to run the same leg of the race. The first runner of this relay usually uses blocks—they carry the starting blocks to the line, crouch down into the starting position, and wait for the gun to fire so the race can begin. I went down to the line to help Eric set up, held his warm-up clothes for him, and tried to help calm his nerves.

That's when I started to notice an internal shift. I had placed those blocks before, in that same spot, multiple times. But being on the *other* side of the blocks was a first for me. Helping the runner—my brother, who I care about a lot—felt good, and even *right*. I can't describe what I was feeling in that moment— the nervousness, the excitement, the realization that I wanted the win more for him than I had ever wanted it for myself.

As the official called the runners to the starting line, I kept repeating one word under my breath, just quietly enough for Eric to hear me: *explode*. Once the runners found their stances, the crowd became silent, and the entire stadium stood still while we waited for that gun to fire. This is the most intense moment for a runner, holding your entire body weight in a couple of fingers, knowing that the slightest muscle twitch could disqualify you.

Then, like a crash of thunder, the gun went off, and Eric was gone. A millisecond after that gun sounded, I jumped to my feet and began screaming, "RUUUUUUN!" I started to yell louder and louder. The entire stadium could hear me, but I didn't care. The passion was coming from somewhere deep within my soul. I began running into the infield, still screaming at the top of my lungs. I must have looked like a crazy person. But I wasn't there for anyone but my brother.

Eric rounded the bend and quickly handed off the baton to his teammate—and just like that, the moment was over.

As I stood there on the infield, I had an epiphany. Something special had just taken place. There wasn't an ounce of competition or comparison with my brother coursing through my veins. This wasn't about me—this was about Eric. Coming alongside him, helping him prepare for the race, being "in his corner" with everything I could bring. And the joy that resulted from that act of serving him blessed me as well.

At a time in my life when my world pretty much revolved around me, I got to set my own agenda aside and serve someone else. I'll never forget the feeling. Looking back on that moment now, it's clear that the Lord was shifting something within me. He was showing me the power of serving another, the joy that comes from putting someone else before yourself. And I will never forget it.

Left on our own, most of us naturally gravitate toward thinking about ourselves first. We instinctively wake up each morning aware of our own wants and needs. It takes a lot of practice and prayer to learn to see in a different way. But if our goal is to build a thriving family, the rhythm of serving—both those within our family and those in our community—is a practice worth cultivating.

Healthy families serve one another. They intentionally cultivate eyes to see the needs of others. When we lead our kids by the example of choosing to serve each other instead of looking for ways to be served, not only are we building the loving family culture we desire, but we're also setting our kids up for a joy-filled life. The greatest joy does not come from winning awards or achieving goals; it comes from the blessing of loving and serving others.

GAIN BY GIVING

What is important is faith expressing itself in love.
GALATIANS 5:6, NLT

Serving requires sacrifice. The choice to serve always costs me something, even if it's small. We want to teach our kids that there is joy and blessing in the sacrifice. When we give up our evening to watch our kids play their favorite sports, we give up our free time, yes; but we also gain the reward of blessing someone we love and cheering them on in doing what *they* love. When our daughter gives up time playing with her favorite toy to give her friend a turn, we want her to learn that the warmth she feels in her heart from choosing to love someone else is the most valuable reward. As Thomas Howard put it:

> Is it not a picture in ordinary terms of what *families*
> are all about; namely, that these few people, thrust
> together and bound by the odd ties of flesh and
> blood, are given the chance to begin to learn the one

big lesson that all men are given to learn—the lesson of Charity? That is, we were made for love, we are commanded to love, and since it doesn't come naturally to us, we have to learn to love. The family situation is, as it were, the elementary schoolroom where we start learning in small, easy, and natural ways to love—that is, to discover that self-giving, freedom, and joy are all one thing.[1]

Each sacrifice of time, each laying down of our own agendas to enter the world of the other, is a movement toward true life. Galatians 5:13 (NLT) tells us, "Use your freedom to serve one another in love." There is a particular freedom that only becomes available to us as we choose to serve—when we, like Christ, choose to live the poured-out life.

ENTER THEIR WORLD

When Jenni was a kid, the roller rink was one of her favorite places. Knowing how much she loved to skate, her mom helped her clear the floor in the garage and turned up the '80s tunes on the boom box. Suddenly Jenni had her very own skating rink! She would skate for hours around that garage floor. To this day, she can't see a pair of roller skates without that memory crossing her mind. I love how Jenni has passed that love of skating on to our girls, and now it's something they all enjoy together.

The little ways we serve our kids matter. And we find out how to do that as we enter their worlds: observing what they love, listening to their unique dreams and desires. In paying attention to our kids' worlds, we can look for insights into how to serve them in ways that would mean the most.

Is there something your child has been asking for your help with that you could make time for? What do they love to do in their free time? Showing them that you're paying attention and that you care about what they enjoy means the world to them. Maybe it's surprising them with a table set up with their favorite activity when they get home from school—slime, playdough, Legos, crafts . . . whatever they're most into right now. Their face will light up when they discover you've taken the time to create an environment for them to do what they love. It *matters*.

Jenni and I had a chance to practice this rhythm just last week with our five-year-old. She had been asking all week to make Christmas ornaments, and we suddenly found ourselves with a rare small chunk of free time, so we decided to try to make it happen for her. We didn't have time to run to the store, so we had to get creative. Jenni grabbed an empty paper towel roll, cut it into strips, and threw the strips on a paper plate with a paintbrush and a blob of glitter glue. I called our daughter to come downstairs.

When she came around the corner and saw the glitter in that glue, you would have thought it was Christmas morning. As she sat next to us, we explained that she could paint each strip with the glitter glue and then we could glue them together to make a snowflake to hang on the tree. I couldn't get over the joy on her face. As she picked up her brush to begin, she looked up at us with those sweet little blue eyes and said, "I can't believe I get to do this!"

The little things. They matter so much! It's impossible to love the people around us well if we care nothing for their world and their loves. Enter their world. Find a simple way to serve your kids this week that would be particularly meaningful to them. The joy it brings will be a lasting blessing to you both.

SERVICE THAT STRENGTHENS

Not all serving is helpful. We want to clarify that we're not talking about the kind of serving that can bring harm to ourselves and to our kids. There's a kind of help that dignifies and inspires, blesses and strengthens; and there's a kind of help that humiliates and belittles, invades, weakens, and can even cause harm. We want to offer our kids the kind of help that strengthens and inspires them, not humiliates, weakens, or even spoils them.

We don't want to get into a habit of doing everything for our kids. If we're too quick to swoop in and "serve" our kids every time a need arises, we can unintentionally rob them of the opportunity to develop those skills on their own. Falling into this rut can not only hinder our kids from growing in their own abilities but also unintentionally foster a sense of entitlement and selfishness.

Sometimes the greatest way we can serve our kids is by giving them the opportunity to learn to do something for themselves. We are wise to listen to the Lord's guidance in order to discern the difference between serving and enabling. Serving should be life-giving, and it should also teach our kids to see those around them and look for ways to serve them as well.

LISTEN TO SERVE
JENNI

Another aspect we've noticed about thriving parents is that they treat their children with great dignity and worth. One of the best ways to serve our kids and to communicate how much we value them is the simple act of *listening* to them and taking their thoughts seriously. It dignifies them. Thriving parents create a culture of dignity in their homes by learning to really *listen* to their kids.

A few years ago, toward the end of 2020, our sweet, introverted nine-year-old asked me to help her with something. The family closeness that resulted from "sheltering in place" during the global pandemic was wonderful at times, but after a while, it also left the introverted souls among us searching for a quiet retreat. She began looking all over the house for a quiet spot where she could read and journal and color all by herself. Girl after my own heart!

She asked me if I could clear out a small space for her in the bottom of our hallway linen closet. We spent a few hours together cleaning out the whole closet and clearing plenty of space for her underneath all the shelves.

"Thank you, Mom!" she said with a wide smile and a huge hug as she looked over her new reading corner. This small act of serving meant the world to her, and all it took was a few hours of my time and attention. The grateful smile on her sweet face was all the reward I needed, but much to my surprise, God had another blessing in mind as well.

Like it may have been for you, 2020 was one of the hardest years we've experienced as a family. The ripple effects of enduring a global pandemic impacted us all in profound, unparalleled ways that we are still sorting through. It was a year of great loss. Big and small. Over and over. "You've got to be kidding me" was a sentence I heard myself saying almost weekly in response to events I would never have chosen. So much loss. One thing after another, the hits just kept coming.

One of the small-yet-big losses for us during that year was the diamond that I looked down to find missing from my wedding ring. We searched high and low all over the house, but to no avail. It had sat safely on my finger for sixteen years, and then that year, of all the years, it disappeared. Another loss.

The day after we created the reading corner, while Averi was reading and coloring to her heart's content, her flashlight illuminated something small and shiny on the carpet below her book. She brought it down to show us, and sure enough . . . it was my diamond.

I couldn't believe it. Something we had completely written off as lost for good showed up. It was a miracle. I found myself saying once more, "You've got to be kidding me." This time in response to something good.

Chris took the diamond to the jeweler's to have it placed securely back in my band, brought it home, and got down on one knee in front of the kids to place it back on my finger. They cheered. I cried, grateful beyond words that God would go out of His way to restore something so small yet so dear to us. God had surprised us.

And I realized something in that moment. What if I had been too busy to listen to Averi's request? What if I had brushed off her heart's desire for a place to enjoy all by herself? The choice to listen to her and to serve her in that moment not only left her feeling loved, seen, and known; it also brought a remarkable blessing my way.

God was getting my attention. It was as if He was showing me that when I choose to put others above myself, to understand their needs and meet them when I can, He rewards it. Sometimes it's with a lost diamond, sometimes it's with the deeper connection that's forged, but serving others is never wasted on Him. "If anyone gives even a cup of cold water to one of these little ones who is my disciple, truly I tell you, that person will certainly not lose their reward" (Matthew 10:42).

LISTEN TO HONOR

Out of the fertile ground of respect, every good thing grows.
AMY GRANT

Listening. I'm working on it. Just a few short minutes of attentive listening can communicate loads of dignity and worth to our kids. The old adage "Children should be seen, not heard" could not be further from the truth. They need to be heard *and* seen. None of us want to communicate to our kids that their thoughts and feelings don't matter or that their dreams and ideas are not worth listening to. But that's exactly what happens when we choose not to listen to them.

Everyone deserves to be listened to. Research shows that people—including young ones—cannot change until they feel listened to. Until they feel understood in some basic way. Feeling heard actually causes us to relax and feel safe. Dr. Henry Cloud notes, "We can't begin to solve problems until there is a sense of trust, and trust is established when we feel listened to."[2] That means before we attempt to correct, we should seek understanding. I have found that if I take the time to listen, often the Lord will show me a different solution than the one I originally planned. Because now I've taken the time to understand, to enter the world of my kids and truly consider *their* ideas as well as my own.

Truly listening to our kids and taking them seriously dignifies them. Watch what happens when you slow down long enough and lean down low enough to give them your full attention. When they come rushing through the door after school, brimming with stories from the day, give their little words the same level of great respect you would give to those coming from your boss. Watch them hold their heads higher and move toward you as they feel truly listened to. It's amazing what a few minutes of active listening can do for our kids. The worth and value this rhythm can shape within them is remarkable. Thriving parents have learned how to listen to their kids.

With our teens, we have learned the more we press, the less they share. The best way to encourage your teens to open up with you is simply to be present and available. I have noticed time and time again, when we are simply faithful to serve them by listening to the small things, eventually they see that they can trust us with the big things. A few minutes of active listening shapes an incredible sense of worth and value in our kids. Thriving parents develop the habit of listening well.

SHOW UP
CHRIS ———————————————————————————

We may not always be able to find the right words or feel like we have much to offer, but we can always serve those we love by showing up. Last week, sitting on some stiff bleachers in a musty gym an hour or so from our house, I saw the power of this principle in effect. I love to watch our son, Kaden, play basketball, so while showing up for his games is not really a sacrifice, it does require rearranging other events to ensure he stays a priority.

During a break in the action, Kaden glanced over at his

mom and me and just smiled. He laughed and mouthed something we couldn't fully understand, but that wasn't the point.
It *mattered* to him that we were there. When his eyes scan the
stands and he finds us there, cheering him on, that's money in
the bank for our relationship. All I had to do was be right there,
in that spot. Serve my son by showing up.

We will all go through seasons when we don't have extra
resources to give, but showing up requires only time and intention. We can all serve those we love through this powerful gift.

Jesus set the ultimate example of showing up. He stepped
down from heaven, spent His time on earth connecting with
people and showing them God's heart, and died a criminal's
death so that you and I could have eternal life with Him. Those
of us who profess Jesus as the Lord of our lives and families are
called to follow in His footsteps and serve others, and showing
up is one of the ways we can do just that.

What follows are some other ways we can create a culture of
serving within our families.

THE BLESSING GAME

Years ago, when our oldest child was in kindergarten, we had
the idea to start the blessing game. Each day, we encouraged
our kids to find a simple way to bless someone. It's amazing
how creative kids can become when you simply turn something into a game. Suddenly, throughout the week, the kids
were running to make each other's beds, finish each other's
chores, and even bring each other their favorite cup of tea at
bedtime. Involve your kids in the blessing game. Ask them
their favorite ways to serve others and what means the most
to them when they're the ones receiving help. Let them use

their creativity. Help them make a colorful chart that lists suggestions of ways to serve. Find a way to make the game fun.

Like any skill, blessing others becomes a habit the more we choose to practice it. It's amazing how God will open our eyes to opportunities to serve when we simply ask for eyes to see them. Years into practicing the blessing game with our kids, out of the blue one week we got an email from our son's teacher. I don't know about you, but anytime a message shows up in my inbox from a teacher, my stomach drops, and I brace myself as I click to open it. You just never know what could be coming your way.

> God will open our eyes to opportunities to serve when we simply ask for eyes to see them.

This email also caused an emotional reaction, but surprisingly, this time it was a good one! It said:

> I just wanted to share a story with you about Kaden . . .
> This morning he came to see me to talk over a class assignment. As he was leaving, he noticed a young man on the floor adjusting some papers (it looked like he had dropped his things maybe). Kaden turned around from the direction he was walking and went up to the young man and said, "Hey! Do you need any help with your things?" The young man declined the help, but I had a proud mama moment on your behalf. Kaden is such a kind young man! It was such a little thing, and yet no one else had thought or cared to stop and ask. Kaden has such great character for such a young man, especially a middle schooler!
> Just thought you would want to know!

Our kids would be the first to tell you that they are far from perfect. But there is goodness within them. There is goodness within your kids too. When we take the time to call it out, to encourage our kids to look for ways to serve others instead of wishing everyone else would notice them, we are giving them the greatest gift.

A purposeful life is a poured-out life. Philippians 2:4 (NLT) says, "Don't look out only for your own interests, but take an interest in others, too." The people who experience the most joy in life are the ones who have chosen to see past their own universe to those around them. Joy comes from serving others.

SERVE TOGETHER

"Pops had knee surgery this week, guys," I casually mentioned to the family as we passed the guacamole around the dinner table. I gave it a minute to see who might pipe up. Our seven-year-old's eyes met mine almost immediately. "Is he okay?" she asked. "Does he need my help?" This is the child who practically came out of the womb serving. Always on the lookout for someone in need of a hero, and always ready to be that hero. "Thanks for asking, babe. He's okay, but he will be in recovery for a while. What are some ways we could help him out while he heals?"

It took a minute, but the ideas started flowing. The little ones got to work making get-well cards, the older girls agreed to help Jenni make one of his favorite meals, and our seventeen-year-old son volunteered to deliver the cards and meal.

Look for opportunities to train your children's hearts in the art of compassion and care. Andi Ashworth notes, "We must create environments where children can grow into creative, kind, and thoughtful adults who know what it looks like to put someone else's needs before their own."[3] Brainstorm as a family ways you could serve together in your community. Is there a single mom who could use a babysitter? A grandparent in need of some company? A local food bank in need of volunteers? Once a month, try out a new idea. Modeling a habit of helping others is one of the greatest gifts we can give our kids.

We all want our kids to become the kind of people who can easily recognize opportunities to serve those around them. We can encourage growth in this area by asking our children questions like these: "Do you remember how it felt to be the new kid in school? What do you wish someone had done to help you feel more welcome? Is there someone in your school you could do that for now?" Or "Who could use a friend at school? Is there anyone who sits alone who you could invite to join you at your table?"

We can offer suggestions to get our kids thinking of ways to serve others, but we need to let them come up with ideas as well and decide which ones to pursue. If we do all the important work of coming up with an idea, purchasing the supplies, and assembling the project, and then we just hand it to our kids to deliver, we're robbing them of the chance to be shaped by the process. Allowing them to serve in their own way, using their own creativity, lets them form the habit for themselves. You'll be amazed by the character growth that results!

PRACTICE

- This week, look for a few ways to serve your kids that would be meaningful to them.

- As a family, brainstorm a list of ways you could serve others in your community. Try a new activity together each month.

- Serve by listening this week. When your kids come home from school, have their favorite snack waiting and let them share about their day.

6

SAYING YES

The Rhythm of Slowing Down

Never say no to your kids' requests to join them....
If you say no too often, they'll stop asking.
MARK AND JAN FOREMAN

Turn my eyes from worthless things,
and give me life through your word.
PSALM 119:37, NLT

JENNI

There are few things better in life than a slow Saturday morning as a kid. The smell of pancakes and bacon cooking on the griddle and the sound of '90s country filling the halls help us all know *Ahhh. It's Saturday.* One of my favorite things about Saturday is the margin it provides to go for a nice long run. One sunny morning, I had just laced up my tennis shoes and headed toward the door. I selected my playlist and slipped in my earbuds. Good to go . . . almost. Just as I opened the front door to head out, I was caught. "Mommy, Mommy, Mommy!! Are you going for a run!?!? Can I go with you? Please, please, pleeeeeeeeease!?!?"

My then nine-year-old daughter looked up at me with those pretty blue eyes and adorable freckles. I paused for a moment. I thought of how much I was looking forward to just tuning out the world for a little while and enjoying the time alone. I thought of all the chores she was supposed to be working on. But in that moment, I also heard another thought: *You get one life.* One Saturday morning in the middle of November to say yes to this beautiful nine-year-old just hungry for a little adventure and some time with her mom. She wasn't begging for a toy or a piece of candy. What she wanted most in this moment was to be with me. So there was really only one answer. I said, "Yes."

Some of life's greatest moments come to us disguised as interruptions.

And you know what? It was the best part of my day. Did I run as fast? Log that extra mile I'd planned on? Burn quite as many calories as I'd wanted? Nope. But I saw a smile as wide as a slice of watermelon across the face of someone I love with my whole heart, and *that* fed my soul. She grabbed her headphones as well, and we danced through the neighborhood mouthing lyrics to our favorite songs along the way. And we came back closer. It was money in the bank for both her heart and mine.

I snapped a few pictures of her along the way because this "Addie smile," as we have come to call it, occurs only when she's having the biggest blast, when the wind is in her face and she's doing something she truly loves. And I couldn't stop staring at it. Couldn't escape the thought that the days are speeding by.

The days when my kids' greatest desire is to be right by my side are fleeting. It reminded me to never say no. Not while I have the chance to say yes.

Some of life's greatest moments come to us disguised as interruptions. Slowing down and saying yes to being present communicates to the person you're with, "I *enjoy* you. There's nowhere else I'd rather be than right here, right now with *you*." It's how strong relationships are built. Love simply cannot grow when we're hurrying through life. The truth is, love only grows when we slow down long enough to cultivate it.

MAKE ROOM FOR SAYING YES

I don't know about you, but sometimes the pace of life can leave me feeling too hurried to savor any of it. Pack the lunches, find the shoes, put away the laundry, answer the question ("Where's my blue shirt?"), clean the soccer cleats, scrub the baseball pants. "Hurry, hurry, everyone! In the car! Grab a snack!"

I can only live this way for so long. After a while, I start to have the nagging feeling that I am just skimming through my life rather than truly living it. The truth is, it's impossible to simultaneously savor life and rush right through it. Savoring life, delighting in it, requires slowing down long enough to fully enjoy it.

I believe in the power of books. I know from experience that God can use a well-timed word to transform a life. Over the years, God has consistently shaped my life through the truth of His Word, through the influence of wise community, and through the power of words on a page.

There were a handful of books I read early in my parenting journey that really changed everything for me. One was called

Never Say No by Mark and Jan Foreman. It was the greatest reminder to me of the importance of relationship with my kids over anything else. And I just couldn't get that advice—never say no—out of my head. The premise behind their encouragement is not permissive parenting, where we say yes to every desire and request from our kids, but rather to always say yes to opportunities to build relationship with our kids.

Over time, God continued to use that encouragement to pull me into all sorts of fun adventures and meaningful moments with my kids. And I noticed almost immediately that my kids' behavior improved when I simply took the time to say yes to them—to enter their world and delight in them there.

Years later, God would also bring these two sages into our lives as real-life mentors and friends. One of the greatest lessons we have learned from Mark and Jan is to slow down and savor our kids. They've taught us that the greatest truth we can impart to our kids is how much we enjoy them.

Slowing down to delight in our kids results in a multitude of rewards. Not only does this rhythm connect me on a deeper level with my children and communicate how much I delight in them, but it also conveys to their young hearts how much *God* delights in them. Over time, they start to receive the message and begin to believe that they are, in fact, people worth delighting in.

The truth is, as the Foremans say, if you keep saying no to the requests of your kids to join them in adventures, eventually, they'll stop asking.[1] Quite a motivating thought. If I keep prioritizing other, more "important" activities and "urgent" tasks over the moments my children are inviting me to enjoy with them, someday they'll give up. No parent wants that.

The key is to remember the glory of the days we are living in, refusing to let anything get in the way of building the strong relationships we want with our kids. Now, I understand that this isn't always possible. There are things we simply must get done. But the point is this: Don't let *anything* steal the gift of knowing and loving your people well. This day, this moment, is the greatest gift. Don't miss it.

STEP INTO THE MOMENT

Saturday has also always been chore day in our house. It's honestly one of my favorite parts of the week: sweet '80s pop filling the halls, vacuums humming, towels wiping, everything getting a proper scrub. Everyone pitches in to do their part (proportionately, of course). Our five-year-old and three-year-old still need quite a bit of assistance, so we work through their rooms together.

One Saturday, as our five-year-old and I rolled pajamas and smoothed sheets, a song began to play over the speakers that was so beautiful it stopped both of us in our tracks. We fell completely silent, instinctively quieting ourselves enough to take in the stunning notes while we worked through our folding. After the song ended, she looked over at me with those gorgeous, gigantic eyes and said, "Mom, I wish I could make a song like that." It was the sweetest moment, and I somehow sensed the choice before me. I could've said something like "That's nice, honey" or "Yes, that was a pretty song, wasn't it?" and moved right along with the next basket of laundry to fold. But I'm working on this slowing down thing—so I heard the prompting: *Step into the moment.*

I paused my folding and sorting, plopped down onto the

floor next to her, and leaned all the way in to ask her more about what she meant.

"You want to write a song?" I asked.

"Yeah, I wish I could make up a song like that and sing it for everyone," she said as her head hit my shoulder.

"Well, let's do it," I said. Her eyes lit up, and she gave me a bright, wide smile. I grabbed my phone, opened voice memos, and hit record. After a few tries, she came up with a pretty little tune to put words to and record. As I played it back for her, her sweet face beamed. She was so proud of herself for the song she had made.

She may never become an award-winning songwriter, tracing her success all the way back to that first moment on the carpet with her mom. Only the Lord knows who she will grow to become. But the connection she and I made in that moment is something that will live on in both of our hearts. The picture she might carry of her mom—who chose to stop what she was doing so she could sit down beside her, to slow down enough to see and listen to her heart. That's a hope worth slowing for.

What I've come to see is that slowing down on its own is not the point. What are we slowing down *for*? We slow down *so that* we can fully lean into what matters most. We slow down to "take hold of the life that is truly life" (1 Timothy 6:19). We choose to slow ourselves down so that we can lean into loving those around us and into the opportunities to strengthen our connection. Slowing down shifts our perspective to see everyday disruptions as invitations to step into the moment.

Dr. Ross Campbell notes, "I found over and over again that my children did not do their best, did not feel their best, and did not behave their best unless I gave them that precious commodity, focused attention."[2] Slowing down means choosing each other. We choose to set aside our own agendas to instead savor the time together.

Some of my favorite moments lately start with someone picking up a ball and heading to the backyard. The sound of that ball bouncing sends out a call to the rest of the house. One by one, the other kids start to trickle down the stairs and into the yard. Chris flips on the café lights, I turn on the music, and suddenly we find ourselves in a golden moment. Balls flying back and forth, one kid swinging on the swing, another flying down the slide, one bouncing on the trampoline, and all of them laughing. When Chris puts his arm around my shoulder, I know what he's going to say: "This is it. It just doesn't get any better than this."

It won't last long, this season we're in. With all seven of us here, living under the same roof, content to simply enjoy time in the backyard together. I don't want to miss a single second of it. I want to say yes to every opportunity I can to slow down and savor each moment.

LET THEM LEAD

When you're a kid, everything is magical. It's a holy rhythm to let our children lead us from their intuitive, sacred sense of slowness. To see the world through their eyes of wonder. To kick off our shoes and run through the grass. To jump into the deep end. To stop and smell the roses.

I'm not naturally inclined to this sacred slowness. I enjoy the satisfaction of feeling productive and working hard. It's a hereditary trait, or so I'm told. My dad is one of the hardest-working humans I know. Most days you can find him up with the sun, and he doesn't stop working until he's "all tuckered out" as the sun begins to set.

Most days, I find my body wants to run at a similar pace. I want to *attack* the day, to pack as much into it as I possibly can. Chores and workouts, laundry and meal prep, running here and there.

Sometimes, though, my focus on getting things done can change the way I see those around me. My body is in constant motion, but my heart is disengaged. Can I dominate the laundry while also listening attentively to my three-year-old's account of her day? Can I speed-clean the living room while also being available for my husband after a long, hard day? And which is more important, completing the chores or connecting with my loved ones?

I'm not saying we should blow off our adult responsibilities to spend the day in bed with our spouse or play make-believe with our kids. Slowing down won't make the chores disappear— but it will keep them from zapping our energy and zest for life and those around us. It can help us find creative ways to connect in the mundane.

Children are never in a hurry. They effortlessly soak up every moment, whether getting lost in the beauty of a starry sky or dancing to the beat of their favorite jam. Adults can discover unexpected new joys when we slow down long enough to see the world through our kids' eyes of wonder.

Just this morning, I let my eight-year-old take the lead. Chris and I were on the front porch, sipping our last few drops of breakfast blend, talking through our plan for the day. Just as we were wrapping up, Kensi rolled up on her bike and said, "Yeah . . . guys, I don't really like that plan." We chuckled and glanced at each other, both feeling very aware of the fullness of the day we'd just discussed and needed to get to. Honestly, everything in me wanted to take advantage of my caffeine buzz and get to work accomplishing my full list for the day. But Kensi's sweet, gigantic blue eyes staring up at me were hard to resist. So instead I leaned low and said, "What would you change about today's plan, love?" To my surprise, all she said was: "I want to go on a walk first with you, Mom."

I could feel my morning to-dos breathing down my neck, yet a smaller, quieter voice seemed to whisper, "Never say no." So I agreed. "Now *that* I can do!" I said. And I let her take the lead.

I faithfully followed my guide as she made a quick loop around the block and then headed to our neighborhood trails. As our feet crossed over from the smooth sidewalk onto the rough terrain of the tree-lined trail, I felt my mood begin to lift. Springtime in Nashville is a glorious sight to behold. The trees are lush, the flowers begin blooming in white, yellow, and pink, and the spring breeze blows through the trees in a way that puts a smile on everyone's face. Everywhere you look, nature takes your breath away.

Kensi must have been feeling the same way because she tugged my shirt and said, "Wow, Mom! Look at all the colors!" I let her take the lead, and she forged ahead with her crooked walking stick in hand, picking flowers and leaves along the way. It was a magical morning. Her sweet little hand in mine, every sentence she uttered beginning with "Did you know . . . ," the way the sunlight shone through her golden-blonde hair—it all made me want to freeze time.

We chatted about the colors we saw and the beautiful

butterflies and birds we spotted. Then, as we rounded the corner to head home, she picked a dandelion for each of us to make a wish on. We took turns blowing the seeds into the breeze and watching them float away. "What'd you wish for, Kens?" I asked. "Well, I'm not supposed to tell you, or it won't come true, but I guess just this once I can," she said. "I wished that we'd remember this moment forever."

The beauty of slowing down is letting ourselves see the world through the eyes of our children, just for a moment. Letting them lead us into the beauty and wonder that they see. It's a transformative practice.

Each moment of saying yes matters. There is so much more brewing beneath the surface of a moment than we can see. When we choose to slow down and step into a special moment with our child, those memories take root deep within their souls and become part of who they are—part of their story. Part of our story as a family.

Our children are extraordinary human beings created in the image of God, who loves them and has a purpose for their lives. Guiding their behavior is important, of course, but even more important is the relationship we pursue with them. Our kids are not animals in need of training to obey our commands. They are more likely to obey us when they feel connected with us. Mark Foreman found that by wrestling with his boys for a little bit every day when he got home from work, by slowing down to be fully present with them, the discipline issues dramatically decreased.[3]

We serve a God who delights in us and accepts us as we

> There is so much more brewing beneath the surface of a moment than we can see.

are, who rejoices over us with singing (Zephaniah 3:17). What would it look like to simply delight in your kids? When was the last time you truly enjoyed just being with them? Had a fun time with them—lecture-free? Let's say yes to the people and moments that matter most, to life that is truly life.

CHRIS ————————————————————————————————

When we intentionally slow down to be present with those we love most, a stronger connection tends to follow. Here are some ideas to get you started.

TAKE A HURRY INVENTORY

Take a family hurry inventory. Which rhythms in your life leave you feeling the most hurried? Call a family meeting and ask each other if there are certain times you are most distracted or rushed. What are some ways you can proactively eliminate hurry and say yes to your family throughout the week? This requires paying attention. Look for clues. Maybe your spouse has already been asking for a date night for months, and all you have to do is make it happen. Maybe your son comes running through the door after school, bursting with stories to tell, and practicing this rhythm looks like turning off your phone and wrapping up any projects before he comes in, readying yourself to be fully present. Are there times you find yourself most distracted or hurried?

When our family did this hurry inventory, we found that dinner was a time we wanted to slow down and be fully present to each other around our table. Screens off, music on, good conversation flowing. Connection. Presence. Life that is truly life.

Another consistent moment of hurry for us was on Sunday

mornings, rushing out the door to church. Flying through the house searching for that missing shoe, brushing hair, arguing over outfits, threatening all manner of consequences to motivate our kids to finally dress and head out the door . . . hurry has a way of bringing out the worst in all of us. We wanted to enjoy our Sundays again. So to combat this weekly rut, we've switched to a later service that allows for more time in the mornings. We also do all the prep work we possibly can the night before to avoid the typical Sunday scramble. It's amazing what just a little more time and intentionality can do.

Talk through your weekly schedule together and note any regular times of hurry or distraction. Are there a few small changes you could make to eliminate hurry from those times? What are some schedule shifts you could make to create more time to slow down together as a family?

TIME AROUND THE TABLE

Family mealtimes can be difficult to fit in around extracurriculars and school activities, but slowing down to connect over a meal has a long-term impact on family culture. Siblings who are close as adults often credit their bond to the meals they enjoyed together around the table every week growing up.

One of the things we love to do each night is take turns to share the day's highs and lows around the table at dinner. This has become a powerful habit for our family. Because they know it's coming, our kids are usually ready with something they've been waiting to share. Sometimes the answers are funny or deep or insightful. Sometimes they are grunts and "It was fine." But we do it anyway. We've been surprised at what's come to the surface during these times. Reserving the time for everyone to say what they need to about their day and listening to them attentively is an important rhythm in our family's culture.

TIME AWAY TOGETHER

Many of the favorite family memories we cherish as adults come from the times we got away together as a family. Something miraculous happens when we load everyone into the car and leave it all behind for just a few days away together. It doesn't really matter where we go. Simply getting that time together, changing up the scenery, and leaving behind the cares of life for a while does something for our souls. And somehow it brings out the best in all of us.

Jenni's family modeled this well. Some of her favorite childhood memories—whether parasailing over the ocean, fishing on a lake in Colorado, or biking down a volcano in Hawaii— were the trips they took together. Her dad put a lot of time and attention into planning each day. As parents in charge of our own family getaways, we can clearly see how much love and effort he put into planning those details. I'm taking notes, Steve!

SPONTANEOUS SLOWING

JENNI

I'm a planner. I appreciate the intentionality of a well-laid plan. In fact, some of my favorite memories happened because we planned them. But I'm also learning that some of the sweetest moments happen in the unexpected. Both are wonderful. Both are needed.

If we embrace time together only when it's planned, we miss out on the magical moments waiting for us in the middle of our ordinary days . . . which is where most of our life is unfolding.

Intentionality and spontaneity enhance each other. A habit of planning special time with my people helps me develop a habit of embracing spontaneous opportunities for time together as they appear. Sometimes the best memories happen when we choose to let go of our well-laid plans.

Every Christmas Eve when I was growing up, my family would attend a candlelight service. It was one of my mom's favorite traditions. The candles, the carols, looking down the aisle to see the whole family together—all of it spoke to her soul. We continued the tradition even after my brother and I each got married and started families of our own. When we come to visit my parents for Christmas, we know to arrive in time for the candlelight service.

One year, as we were all getting ready for the Christmas Eve service, the news came that my brother and sister-in-law's flight had been delayed. They would not arrive in time. We had a choice: We could go ahead and miss having them with us, or we could stay back and wait for them to arrive.

We let my mom make the final call; no one wanted to deprive her of her favorite Christmas custom. Although she was sad to miss the candlelight service, staying home and being together as a family ultimately won out. When my brother and his wife finally arrived, the kids were already in bed, so the rest of us headed outside to enjoy some time around the fire. I don't remember exactly how it happened, but someone started singing a Christmas carol, and slowly we all joined in. After a few more songs, someone else offered up a prayer, and then we each shared something we'd learned that year and something we wanted to work on in the year to come.

We chose to embrace the disruption and to prioritize

connection over our well-laid plans. And it was the sweetest Christmas Eve service we'd ever had. Cozied up under the stars, catching someone's eye as we sang our favorite carols, sharing deep conversation . . . it all meant the world to us. Because none of our individual family units lived in the same city at that time, experiences like this one, of sharing our hearts around a crackling fire, were few and far between. It felt like a rare and beautiful gift. And a new favorite tradition was born for us all. Some of the sweetest moments can happen in the unexpected if we keep our hearts open to receive them.

LIFE THAT IS TRULY LIFE

From time to time in our neighborhood, I see an older man pushing his precious grandbaby along in a gray stroller. For some reason, seeing them together always takes me by surprise. Grandpas are not normally the ones you see trotting along behind strollers in neighborhoods. As I pass him on my morning jog, he smiles, as if he knows a secret. I think perhaps he does. He's delighting in the sweet gift of his grandbaby while the rest of the world hustles and bustles around him. Perhaps that is the gift of getting older: The clarity of what matters most allows us to enjoy the truest gifts life has to offer. No more ladders to climb, ambitions to chase, portfolios to build. Just life to savor.

It reminds me of one of my favorite verses, 1 Timothy 6:19: "So that they may take hold of the life that is truly life." The beautiful Greek word translated "take hold," *epilambanomai*, means "to lay hold of or to seize upon anything with the hands," and it can also mean "to rescue one from peril" and "to help."[4] It's the same word used to describe Jesus' action as he scooped

Peter out of the rushing waves and said, "You of little faith, why did you doubt?" (Matthew 14:31).

As we shift our attention to that which matters most, is it possible that Jesus is helping us enact a rescue we so desperately desire? When we take hold of that which God deems essential, refusing to let the distractions and hurry of the world pull our gaze away, we might feel the extended hand of Jesus helping us pull our truest lives out of the waves threatening to consume them.

We all long for more life. Not more activity. Not more events to rush to or responsibilities to juggle. But more of the life that is truly life. What our souls desperately long for is more *zōē*, the Greek word translated as "life" in 1 Timothy 6:19. *Zōē* often refers to "life real and genuine, a life active and vigorous, devoted to God, blessed."[5] When we fix our gaze on Jesus, the Source of life, we open ourselves up to experience the rich, fulfilling life that is only found in Him.

Let the world around us clamor and compete to be the best, to have the best, to look the best . . . while you and I pursue a deeper life of slowing down. A life of surrender and substance. A life that is truly life.

PRACTICE

- What pushes you toward hurry in your life? Why?

- Keep a running list—in a journal or on your phone—of times during your week when you notice hurry creeping in. What are some ways you can proactively eliminate hurry from those areas of your life?

- Carve out a night this week to enjoy time around the table as a family. Encourage everyone to share their highs and lows from the day or to name something that's their favorite.

- Say yes to the next invitation from your child to connect. I bet it will be the sweetest part of your day.

- Be on the lookout this week for opportunities to slow down and step into the moment.

7

LIFE ON THE EDGE

The Rhythm of Seeking Adventure

Awaken your spirit to adventure;
Hold nothing back, learn to find ease in risk;
Soon you will be home in a new rhythm,
For your soul senses the world that awaits you.
JOHN O'DONOHUE

CHRIS

One of our favorite things to do each summer is sneak away, just Jenni and me, to one of the most beautiful places on the planet: Lake Tahoe. There's just something about that combination of majestic mountains, tall California redwoods, and crystal-clear water that feels like paradise to us. We bask in the flow of uninterrupted time together: float the Truckee River, grab lunch on the back deck at the Sunnyside Café, and splash in the freezing water at the basin of Emerald Bay. It's heaven.

While away, we always dream about how amazing it would be to one day bring the kids along to experience this breathtaking place. Well, this past winter, the opportunity miraculously came knocking. Through a work trip I was taking near Tahoe and a ton of airline points saved up, we managed to pack up the entire Graebe crew and fly west for a little family adventure at Lake Tahoe.

It was winter, which of course is very different from the sunny summer days we were used to, but even covered in piles of snow, it was still a breathtaking place to explore! The week we chose to visit just happened to be during the heaviest snowfall on record—*ever*! Over the five days we were there, we saw more than four feet of snow hit the ground. Of course, the kids loved every minute of it. The little ones made all the snowmen they could muster, we cooked dinner at the cabin and played games as a family by the fire, and we all just enjoyed the slow together!

One particular moment from this trip turned out to be an adventure none of us will ever forget. Obviously, when in Tahoe with record snow, you hit the slopes. We had heard rumors that the mountain might close because of all the snow it had received overnight, so we knew the window to hit the slopes might close on us. We quickly got the littles dropped at ski school, popped on the skis, buckled in the snowboards, and hit the mountain.

After a glorious morning on the mountain, seeing the teens fly by us here and there, it was getting close to lunch, and we decided to squeeze in just one more long run. Now, we had never skied this mountain before, but as far as we could tell from the map, it looked as though the longest runs were all on the east side. We decided to head up the mountain on a trail we hadn't tried before, but as we slid into our place in line, Jenni leaned over to ask me, "Are you *sure* this is a blue run and not a black? There aren't very many people in this line, and I don't see any kids riding this lift." Seeing kids on a lift is usually a pretty good indicator that you aren't about to put yourself in harm's way and potentially meet your Maker. As I glanced back at the map, I swear I saw two paths at the top: One way was clearly blue and the other black. So with confidence I responded, "Oh yeah, babe. There's a blue at the top for sure. We'll be fine." So we jumped on the lift and headed toward the top.

As we exited the chairlift and rounded the corner, we knew immediately that we were in trouble. Glancing down at the paths before us, we saw there was not a single trail that was not literally straight down. We looked high and low for that little blue sign, but no luck—there were only steep blacks as far as the eye could see.

This was also the absolute top of the mountain, so the temperature must have been at least ten degrees colder than down at the lodge, and the winds were whipping so hard you could barely breathe. Now, this alone was enough to scare the you-know-what out of us, but we noticed yet another cause for alarm scattered along the side of the mountain: poor, hopeless skiers and snowboarders just sitting there, stuck in mounds of miserable powder. Some seemed as if they had given up on life altogether and decided this was it: They had found their final resting place. Others would kick and fight to move their bodies, only to get stuck deeper and deeper. At this point, we really had no choice. The only way back to our kids and to the warmth of that ski lodge was down this black-diamond demon.

My brave, adventurous wife decided to go first. Just before she took off, some British dude on skis who must have seen the terror on her face passed by her and said, "Traverse! Traverse! Turn your skis sideways across the mountain, and you'll be fine!" It seemed like good enough advice, so that's what Jenni did. At first, she was nailing it, and hope began to rise in my soul that this wasn't as bad as it looked, and that she might in fact forgive me for leading her to this crazy trail. Until suddenly, the traverse guy's advice stopped working. I watched in horror as my poor, beautiful wife began to gain momentum down the steep slope and found herself flying headfirst into multiple feet of fresh powder.

It was the oddest experience, watching all this unfold. A few thoughts hit my mind all at once. First, I knew I was *definitely* dead. Second, there was nothing I could do to help her— and third, more than likely, a similar fate awaited me as well. "You okay, babe?" I shouted, to no avail. All I could do in that moment was pray and hope that she would be able to get out of this snow so that one of us could be there to raise our children. Luckily, Jenni is a pro. She was able to wiggle herself up onto her skis and, eventually, to freedom. I cannot even begin to tell you the level of relief that came over me as I saw her finally find her way down that mountain.

I then realized I had to try my hand at this snow-filled gauntlet as well. So I jumped up on my board and took the ride. Before I knew it, I began to pick up too much speed, and then *boom* . . . I bit it so hard that I went tumbling deep into the snow. I'd been in powder before, but nothing like this. Every move I made to get myself out only made things worse. After quite a few minutes of fighting for footing, I was able to free myself to get a little further down the mountain . . . only to hit the powder again.

Once I finally hit snow that had been groomed and knew I wasn't destined to spend the rest of my life trapped in the snow in my favorite place on earth, a massive wave of relief washed over me, and I was able to find my way down to safety.

And then I saw her . . . and she saw me, and we ran to each other like we were in one of those cheesy movies. Sort of. I wish I could say the birds were chirping, but they weren't. They were probably frozen to death somewhere on the mountain because of the arctic temps. Our hair wasn't whipping in the wind with a beautiful melody playing behind us. It was more like frozen snot bubbles all over my face. But even with all that, wrapped in way too many layers of clothes, we hugged each other a little tighter than usual in that moment. Just grateful beyond words to be safe, alive, and out of the snow.

As we stumbled into the lodge, we immediately saw our fourteen-year-old daughter, who came clunking toward us with flushed cheeks and a wild look on her face. "I just went down the craziest black run of my life!" she said. She began telling us how she and Kaden had gotten stuck on the same black-diamond powder run as we had. They had both snowboarded before, but it had been years. For two teenagers who had never seen anything like it, taking snowboards into deep powder was a recipe for disaster.

It was the craziest thing, though. As Addie unpacked the story for us, I could hear her nerves start to calm, and she could not stop smiling. She kept repeating one line—"That was the hardest thing I've ever done in my life"—but with a smile that conveyed a deep sense of confidence in herself for making it out of there alive.

As Addie continued to unpack the story, Kaden entered through the left lodge doors, and a deep wave of relief came over all of us. "Kaden!" we all exclaimed and ran to hug him, glad he had made it out of there alive. In typical teenage-boy fashion, one of the first things out of his mouth after "Man, that was crazy!" was "Can we get some food? I'm starving!" In that moment we knew he was going to be fine.

As we shared our "war stories" together over lunch in the lodge that day, something important was happening. We could all feel it. It was one of those magical moments where we found our forty-two-year-old selves sitting almost as peers with our teenage kids. Just four Graebes recapping the wild and wondrous adventures of the day! Exactly the way it should be. And it remains one of my all-time favorite moments with our teenagers.

> There's a particular strength available to us on the other side of a great adventure, a strength that nothing else can create.

In that one moment, with our cheeks still flush from the wind of a fresh adventure, having all just overcome something we never would have thought we could, something we never would have chosen to go through on our own, we all sat a little taller. There's a particular strength available to us on the other side of a great adventure, a strength that nothing else can create. The experience of it bonded us in a deeper way. "I'm going to grab some hot chocolate!" Addie announced as she headed toward the café. After a few steps, she paused and turned back around. "Do you want some too, Mom?" she said thoughtfully to Jenni.

Adventure brings out the best in us. It fills our souls with life and draws us closer to each other, connecting us over shared experience. It develops greater character in us and draws out new strengths from deep within us.

One thing we have noticed time and time again to be a consistent part of thriving families around us is this rhythm of seeking adventure. And not just the flying-down-the-mountain kind. This rhythm of adventure is more of a mind-set of adventure—one that's always looking out ahead toward growth and change.

So many incredible families have gone before us and paved the way, modeling what life can look like as we say yes to the Lord and take our kids along on the great adventures He invites us into. As we refuse to grow comfortable and complacent but instead choose to play a vital role in the new thing God is doing, showing our kids what a life of adventure looks like. Thriving families say yes to the new adventures the Lord is calling them into.

The truth is, we're all wired for adventure. No one wants to look back on the life they lived still holding on to a long list of things they wish they had done. We all want to look back and marvel at the incredible experiences we enjoyed together as a family. As Eugene Peterson wrote in *Run with the Horses*, "The aim of the person of faith is not to be as comfortable as possible but to live as deeply and thoroughly as possible—to deal with the reality of life, discover truth, create beauty, act out love."[1] A thriving family culture will include embracing plenty of beautiful adventures together.

Think through the adventures you've taken together as a family over the years. What was the last great adventure you said yes to? What great joy came as a result? What lessons did you learn on the other side of the experience? How did you grow individually and together as a result of saying yes?

Adventures are a pathway to joy. What we have experienced through our own adventures as a family, both big and small, is that there is a certain level of joy and life that shows up on the faces of our kids that can only be seen in the midst of a great adventure. We call it the joy smile. There's just something about mustering up the courage to go for something new that fills our souls with fresh life, and time and time again, it shows up on our kids' faces. Whether it's trying out a new skill, jumping off the cliff at the lake, sledding down that hill, or going for a new dream, cultivating a mindset of adventure keeps us awake and alive and opens us up to experience the greatest parts of life—together.

And of course, adventure looks wildly different for each of our kids. Each child has different dreams, different passions, and different personalities. One of our kids has been a wild adventurer since birth. She'll look up, breathless from her latest thrill, and invite me to join in: "You do it with me!" That little phrase has pulled me in, usually reluctantly, to join her in all manner of adventures—from jumping through waterfalls, to running through backyard sprinklers in the middle of March, to riding a roller coaster called Blazing Fury! Our kids can lead us into the most incredible experiences if we let them.

The world becomes a fresh, new place to us when we begin to see it through their eyes. Make time for adventures that bring out the inner child in you and in your older kids if you have them. Roll down that grassy hill. Race bikes together around the neighborhood. All kinds of adventures open up to us as we let our kids lead us into the world they see.

Eugene Peterson said, "People [including little ones] are not problems to be solved. They are mysteries to be explored."[2] Each day, our kids are becoming something new. Exploring adventure gives us a front-row seat to watching our kids grow and change and discover their own unique passions and callings along the way. We get to look for the joy that flashes across their faces as they discover something they love. We get to encourage the gifts we see growing within them. We get to gently push them out of the nest and into brave new things. We get to watch as they begin to spread their wings and fly. We get to remind them to stand back up when they fall down and offer them a safe place to land when they come back home.

LIFE ON THE EDGE

There's a legendary John Muir story Eugene Peterson told as a metaphor for a life of adventure in Christ. Muir, an early American explorer, nature writer, and preservationist, has often been called "the patron saint of the American wilderness."[3] "For decades he tramped up and down through our God-created wonders," Peterson recalled, "from the California Sierras to the Alaskan glaciers, observing, reporting, praising, and experiencing—entering into whatever he found with child-like delight and mature reverence." While Muir was visiting a friend's cabin one winter day, a wild storm settled upon the valley. Instead of taking shelter in the cozy cabin to ride out the storm, Muir decided to run straight *into* the storm, scrambling his way to the top of a Douglas fir to fully take it in, in all its wind-whipped glory. My man!

This image of Muir had a profound impact on Peterson. He wrote:

> The story of John Muir, storm-whipped at the top of the Douglas fir in the Yuba River valley, gradually took shape as a kind of icon of Christian spirituality for our family. The icon has been in place ever since as a standing rebuke against becoming a mere spectator to life, preferring creature comforts to Creator confrontations.[4]

"A mere spectator to life"—a thought that makes me shudder. No one wants to look back on their one God-given life and feel as though they had merely watched it all unfold from the sidelines, clinging to their comfort instead of stepping out courageously to experience it completely. We want to live life to the *full*—to follow Jesus' lead into the wild adventures He calls us to. We want to lead the kind of life our kids could long to emulate in their wildest dreams. That kind of life requires moving out of our comfort zones and saying yes to new adventures.

Growth requires change. When we stop changing, we stop living. Thriving together requires that we keep saying a wholehearted yes to the adventures God invites us into.

There is no growth without risk. As Margaret Guenther warns us, "How easy it is to shrink from risk, to let our hearts and minds grow small and constricted instead of bold and expansive."[5] Life becomes very small when we refuse to move past our comfort zones.

Some of the healthiest families we've encountered have fully embraced this mindset of adventure. As they seek adventure together, they practice holy attentiveness to the work that God is up to around them and look for ways to join Him in it.

Which experiences and habits bring you the most life? What activities stir your heart and make you feel most alive? What would it look like to lean into those rhythms? To make space for daily and weekly touchpoints of those experiences in your life together? Here are some thoughts on practical ways we can begin to cultivate this rhythm of adventure in our families.

WATER THEIR DREAMS

An important part of cultivating this mindset of adventure in your family is discovering and supporting each other's dreams.

Sit down with each kid this week and ask them what they are dreaming of most right now. What ideas or activities are rising to the top of their hearts? Maybe they want to try out for the school play or learn to ride a horse, or perhaps they want to start a club for new kids at school or write a novel someday. Encouraging our kids to go for some of these dreams helps them develop the bravery and confidence they will need to live a robust life.

Some kids will have no trouble answering this question. What *aren't* they dreaming of? What experiences *don't* they want to try? They will tell you *all* the things! For others, it may take a bit more discussion to help them discover their dreams.

Another way to ask this question is "If you could change anything in your life right now, what would it be?" I often use this question to trick my wife into pinpointing her dreams! This query might be easier to answer for some people. Most of us have no trouble knowing at least a few changes we'd like to make, and most of the time those desires for change point to a dream worth pursuing. Write them down together.

It's important to water those seeds by encouraging your kids to lean into the adventure pursuing their dreams entails. What are some things you could do this month to help them take at least one step toward that change? What's one obstacle in the way of bringing that dream to life? Discuss as a family how you could get behind each other's dreams.

Maybe your child's dream is to try out for the school musical, and watering that dream looks like signing them up for music lessons to prepare for the audition or watching the musical together as a family. Maybe their dream is to start a bracelet business in the neighborhood; watering that dream might mean helping them learn how to make a budget and set a price for their products. There are so many ideas and dreams our kids can come up with. As parents, it's our job to get behind those dreams and help bring them to life.

When our kids are in this discovery stage, it's important to give them all sorts of things to try out. Expose them to different kinds of experiences. They may be unaware of a gifting, ability, or passion simply because they haven't been exposed to it yet. One friend of ours cut out images of all different kinds of activities from books and magazines and glued them onto a poster board, and then she invited her kids to circle the activities that looked exciting to them. Get creative in finding ways to peek into your kids' souls to see what dreams and desires and bents are there. Find ways to draw them out. Ask God to open your eyes to see the giftings and callings he has placed on your kids. And then proactively look for ways to cultivate those things.

PERMISSION TO CHANGE

JENNI ——————————————————————————

Chris and I are mountain, lake, forest, cabin people. Given a choice, we will pick a cabin in the woods overlooking a quiet stream over almost anything. But God gave us five children who adore the beach. It is their happy place. Every time we go, Chris and I marvel at how much time they can spend there, completely content with the sand and the waves. They will stay as long as we let them, and anytime we vote on a family trip, the kids' vote is always unanimous: beach!

Part of me longs for at least one of our kids to appreciate the beauty of a forest cabin with me. I have gone to great lengths to persuade them. We've taken countless hikes through the prettiest trails I can find. And still, our kids prefer the beach.

Somewhere along the way, healthy parents realize their children are not there to become just like them but to become who God made them to be. We need to provide room for our kids to try on new things to see what fits *them*. To become the beautiful, unique creatures God has designed them to be—even when that looks different from us.

This is often easier said than done. We say, "Be whatever you want to be," but we put a baseball in the crib or ballet shoes on the dresser. We carry our own dreams for our children in our hearts. But the truth is, God lovingly designed each one of us with unique giftings and callings. One of my favorite verses in Jeremiah says, "Before I formed you in the womb I knew you" (Jeremiah 1:5). He knew us . . . each one of us. Before God formed us, He picked out our unique makeup. Our job as parents is to help our children discover the incredible things

God has planted inside them; the unique, wonderful way He has made them.

TRUST THE STORY GOD IS WRITING

Having their own sets of ideas, preferences, and dreams goes to an even deeper level in the teenage years. There is a motto Chris and I have adopted while raising adolescents: Trust the story God is writing. God is always up to something new, and the story He is writing for our kids is greater than anything we can imagine. Some of the adventures He invites our kids into might stretch us as parents.

Say yes to the bigger story God has for your children. And for your family. Their dreams may not be your dreams. We can always trust the story He is writing, even when it looks different from what we expected. Even when it pushes us outside our comfort zones. God knows our kids and loves them even more than we do, and they belong to Him. *Trust the story He is writing.*

This requires humility—a key component in embracing our growing children and a common characteristic we've noticed of great parents. Marked humility. Humility reminds us: This is not about us. This remarkable, made-in-the-image-of-God human I've been entrusted with raising is not an extension of me or my dreams and desires. She is a beautiful, unique person all on her own. Humility empowers us to give her permission to grow and change —and to be her greatest cheerleader along the way. A humble heart moves beyond wanting to reproduce myself to truly desiring much more for my kids. Humility prays that they will do even greater things than I have done.

Pushing our agenda on our kids, making their lives all about us, can stunt their flourishing as unique individuals. A humble heart gives others freedom to fly. Humility points us toward opportunities to disciple our kids in the unique dreams and callings God has for their lives. Our identity comes from the Lord, not our kids. When we live confidently from that place, it frees us to trust His plans for our kids and embrace each plot twist along the way.

FREEDOM TO FLY

A recurring theme in my life since I married this man almost twenty years ago has been what feels like Chris and the Lord conspiring to continually push me out of my comfort zone. But here's what I've learned about life on the other side of saying yes to things that scare you: It's where the best life is found. As John O'Donohue wrote, "A life that continues to remain on the safe side of its own habits and repetitions, that never engages with the risk of its own possibility, remains an unlived life. There is within each heart a hidden voice that calls out for freedom and creativity."[6]

Part of living out this rhythm of adventure involves gently nudging our kids out of the nest when they're ready and allowing them opportunities to stretch their wings. Some will want to cling to the nest, while others will seem like they were born ready to fly. This will happen in many ways throughout their lives, many times before *we* feel ready. As parents, it's our job to recognize the opportunities as they arise.

In the early days of family life, when our kids were all really small (and our budget as well), one of our favorite weekend family rhythms was grabbing a five-dollar pizza and heading to the park to play or back home to enjoy a movie night. One particular week, Chris was out of town, so just the kids and I went to pick up our pizza. When we pulled up to the restaurant, Kaden—just seven years old at the time—turned to me and asked, "Mom, can I go in and grab the pizza?" It was dark and starting to rain. As a young mom I was still really cautious, so I said, "I don't know, bud. It's raining pretty hard out there." Such a small thing, going in to pick up a pizza, but for a seven-year-old boy longing to step into Dad's shoes, it may as well have been climbing Mount Everest. This was something he would watch Chris do, and I knew that was part of the reason he wanted to try it on his own so much. "Please, Mom," he pleaded. "I can do it!"

I heard John Eldredge's words echoing in my head. *He is asking you, "Do you think I have what it takes to be a man?"*[7] I knew this was the first of many times Kaden would unknowingly ask that question of us. This was a small but important adventure I could say yes to.

I handed him the money, told him what to say to the man behind the counter, and watched his precious eyes light up. "Got it! Thanks, Mom!" And off he went. I watched as Kaden ran inside and took his place in line. His sweet little eyes could barely see over the cash register as he placed our order and handed the man his cash. He looked back at me with a smile and a thumbs-up that said, *See, Mom? I got this.* As he walked back to the car, pizza in hand, his face was full of pride that he had what it took to step into his dad's shoes. *Yes, you do, Kaden. You sure do.*

These seemingly small moments are where character begins to grow. Where the virtues we pray our kids will develop begin to take shape. Confidence and courage, compassion and kindness. These virtues only take root in our kids on the other side of venturing out on their own. Say yes to their dreams, both big and small. To the bigger story God is writing. Say yes to the God of adventure, and watch as He grows stronger hearts within them on the other side.

This rhythm of adventure, of letting our kids take risks and discover their own capabilities, comes easier to Chris than it does to me. Chris lives in this rhythm: following his instincts, taking risks, learning from his mistakes, and charging ahead. Care and warmth, nurture and comfort—these rhythms come naturally for me. Saying yes to risk? Not as much. I'm working on it. What I am learning, though, is that there is so much life out there God is calling our kids to live. Calling *us* to live together. I don't want any of us to miss it! The more I say yes to our kids' requests to try new things, even those outside our comfort zones, the more I find the incredible reward waiting for us on the other side. Sometimes that reward is great joy; sometimes it's the opportunity to learn a hard lesson. Both are a blessing. Thriving parents learn to lean into adventure—and to give their kids the freedom to fly.

PRACTICE

- When was the last time you felt completely alive?

- What was the last great adventure you said yes to as a family? What great joy came as a result?

- What lessons did you learn on the other side of the experience? How did you grow individually and together as a result of saying yes?

- This week, ask each family member what some of their deepest dreams are in this season. Think of ways you can begin watering their dreams and watching them grow.

- As a family, brainstorm a handful of new things you've each been wanting to try. Make it a goal to try at least one per month.

8

THIS IS IT

The Rhythm of Staying in Awe

Enjoy the little things, for one day you may look back
and realize they were the big things.

ROBERT BRAULT

JENNI

I have a confession. Yesterday, I ignored all the experts' advice and went digging through my seventeen-year-old's closet. Initially, I wandered my way in, looking for a set of missing sheets I was sure must be hiding somewhere underneath those piles of clothes. (He keeps his room pretty neat most of the time except for that crazy closet.) As I dug through the mounds of clothes and shoes, I heard all the wise parenting experts echoing in my head, reminding me not to clean my kids' closets for them. "If you do, they'll never learn to do it for themselves," they preached.

I agree. Which is why I have obediently complied and not stepped foot in his closet for years. But for some reason, on this day, I pushed right past their advice and kept on going.

And I just let myself go all in. I don't know what came over me. Organizing and straightening to my heart's full content. I sorted the dirty clothes from the clean, hanging each T-shirt and sweatshirt from the stack, and . . . ahh. It felt *so* good. Not just because I could finally see the floor, either. As I lifted each item, I felt a deep sense of awe and gratitude for my son come rushing in, right there where I least expected it, and I gave myself permission to just let it come.

How did these clothes get so big? I thought, over and over. Flashes of closets gone by kept flooding my mind. It used to be Lightning McQueen T-shirts and Thomas the Tank Engine pajamas. Now somehow I found it filled with favorite sports teams and Nike swooshes. How did we get here so fast? Oh, the joy it has been, loving and raising this kid under my roof. I can't believe he is *seventeen* now. Just yesterday I was holding his tiny face in my hands.

And then the tears came. *I don't want it to end,* I thought as my knees hit the floor. It seems like a cruel trick, to become so attached to someone and love them so much, knowing you will one day have to let them go. *I don't want to let him go, Lord,* I confessed. I am so proud of him. So grateful to know him. So *changed* by the gift of raising him. *Lord, I trust the story you're writing. For each one of us individually and for us together as a family. I know, I know—you know the plans you have for us . . . to prosper us and not to harm us, to give us a hope and a future.*

I trust you. I know you will carry him and cover him just as you always have. You will be faithful again tomorrow just as you have been today. But ahh, it's just so hard to let him go!

I did what I often do when feeling this way: I went to see an older, wiser friend to seek some wisdom on this whole "letting go" thing. She has launched two children into adulthood, and her words have always been a source of encouragement for me, so I couldn't wait to settle in with my coffee, cozy up on her front porch in the woods, and soak up all the wisdom.

"We think we carry our kids for nine months," she said, "but the truth is, we carry them for much longer—until we get them to a place of *being* carried." Her words reminded me that the God who gave these precious kids to me, entrusting them to my care, knows every single day He has planned for them. He knows every hair on their heads. His love for them is far beyond my own; His story for them is far greater than anything I could possibly imagine. He will carry them always. Even after they leave our homes. And He will carry us as we send them off and cheer them on as they fly.

The truth is, ultimately, we *do* want to let our kids go. The whole goal of this parenting thing is to successfully raise fully functioning adults who will go out into the world and make a difference. So the most loving thing we can do for them is slowly let them go, bit by bit over the years, until they're capable of flying without us. What a gift, to cheer them on as they fly!

As I sat there on my friend's porch, the Lord began to gently whisper, "Your relationship with Kaden is not ending. It's just taking on a new shape." Parenting never ends. We will always be our children's parents. It's a sacred, covenant relationship that goes on forever. It changes over the years, just as we do, but it never ends. If we trust the story God is writing, we can offer our deepest thanks for the season that was and embrace the joy awaiting us in the season to come. The key is how we choose to see this transition. "What a gift," my friend said, "to give a proper thanks for the end of one glorious season and to lean into the beauty of the next."

Awe invites us to see the world through fresh eyes of wonder. It's all about how we see.

Every morning we have a choice: to enjoy the day or merely survive it. To view our family as a remarkable gift we've been given or as a fixed part of our ordinary life. We can receive each new day with joy and gratitude as a fresh opportunity to know our spouse and kids in all their complexity and depth, or we can believe the lie that we already know everything there is to know about them. The choice is ours. Awe invites us to see the world through fresh eyes of wonder. It's all about how we see.

> Our goal should be to live life in radical amazement . . . [to] get up in the morning and look at the world in a way that takes nothing for granted. Everything is phenomenal; everything is incredible; never treat life casually. To be spiritual is to be amazed.
>
> ABRAHAM JOSHUA HESCHEL

In all our study of great parents over these past few years, I've realized something. Though each of these five rhythms is present in some form within their family life, there is one rhythm that seems to rise to the very top. In fact, it's almost as if the other rhythms flow freely from this one foundational practice. Over the years, these parents cling to the truth that having a family to love and raise is a sacred, holy, remarkable gift. And they *treasure* it. You can see the fruit of it all over their lives. Through all different types of days. In the mountaintop moments and the valley-deep hours, they remain profoundly grateful. They choose to stay in awe.

Awe is that deep sense of wonder, joy, and gratitude that takes us by surprise, a movement toward admiration and inspiration. Moments of awe shatter our expectations, stop us in our tracks, and take our breath away. Whether it's going for a walk in the woods, taking in a glowing sunset, or watching a parent with their newborn baby, everyday awe can reignite us—if we pause to let God capture our attention. The truth is, we are all wired for awe. God created us with the ability to marvel at the world He made, the moments He allows us to experience, and the relationships He gives us to cherish. Awe is set deep within our bones, in our image-bearing humanity—something we were meant to experience on a regular basis.

Awe is about staying open to moments of holy, no matter how small. As philosopher and civil-rights leader Howard Thurman said, "There must be always remaining in every man's life some place for the singing of angels, some place for that which in itself is breathlessly beautiful."[1]

Practicing awe requires a posture of gratitude. In relationships and in life, gratitude involves remembering the miracle of being alive and choosing to view every day as a gift instead of a given. I *get* to wake up every day next to my spouse; I *get* to be the mom of these five incredible kiddos; I *get* to live in my favorite city in the world—and even when things are far from perfect, even when a day doesn't go according to plan, it's all still a gift. I can still make space for this practice of gratitude and awe. Healthy parents model a life of gratitude.

Practicing awe shapes us into a certain kind of person. A person who can recognize the beauty in any moment (even the difficult ones) and in the people around us (even in their worst moments). Thriving families remember that being together under one roof is a gift for only a short season—a season worth cherishing. Each day, each moment together is to be treasured and enjoyed and stewarded well. Like flowers that bloom and wither, we are here for just a moment, and we have the incredible blessing of being a family. When our lives are over, we were here, *together*. What a gift.

THE GIFT OF TODAY
CHRIS ————————————————————————

Teach us to number our days,
that we may gain a heart of wisdom.
PSALM 90:12

I love how Psalm 90:12 says, "*Teach* us to number our days." It doesn't come naturally; we need to be *taught*. Numbering our days means remembering they are a gift from God and that before we know it, they will all be gone. John O'Donohue had it right when he wrote, "We dodder through our days as if they were our surest belongings. No day belongs to us. Each day is a gift."[2] This mindset empowers us to live intentionally, to see the inherent sacredness of this life and this family we are building and to say yes to what truly matters.

What would change in how we walk through life if we woke up each day and chose to see it as the precious gift that it truly is?

Over the past year or so, a fun new ritual has formed within our weekly family rhythms. As a family of seven, we are often out and about on weeknights, running our kids from one activity to the next: play practice, soccer practice, baseball games . . . you get the idea. So we often find ourselves shuffling around town in the early evening hours, typically around sunset. Recently, our eight-year-old has become fascinated with the glory of a painted sky around dusk. She is often the one in the car to break us out of our hurried focus with a not-so-subtle "Wow! Look at those colors!" or "Guys, you have to see this sky!"

Pausing to appreciate a beautiful sunset is something we should all prioritize. But one of the greatest gifts has been to take in these sunsets through the wondrous eyes of our eight-year-old. She has this unique ability to see through the colors and recognize the hand of God painting every hue and stroke of the magnificent sky. Her eyes are open wide, and it's as if she is riding on those clouds. It's clear that she is filled with awe and wonder in these moments and keenly aware that she will never see that specific sunset with that exact design ever again. She invites us all to lean in with her and experience the fullness of it.

I'm learning a lot from Kennedi on how to see the world. Unlike adults, who can get so caught up in the stresses of life that we miss out on wonder, she easily recognizes beauty all around her. She leans into awe, and—thankfully—she brings us with her.

The rhythm of staying in awe isn't about following a step-by-step formula; it's about taking a heart posture. We can model for our kids—and they can model for us!—what practicing awe looks like. It's about noticing the big hidden within the small, the great blessings and beauty of everyday life.

Our kids might recognize on their own that a sunset is breathtaking or a waterfall is beautiful, but it's our job as parents to connect their hearts to the Source of all beauty. To remind them of the brilliant Creator who made all awe-inspiring sights. As pastor and author Paul David Tripp says, "Every created awe is meant to point you to the Creator."[3] The same God who spoke the mountains, oceans, and sunsets into existence also created each of our children. Not one other person among the eight billion humans on this globe has the same fingerprints as them. We can foster a sense of awe and wonder in our kids by helping them make those important connections.

> Moments of awe will become the memories we cherish most.

If we let them, our kids can lead us into a deeper level of awe and wonder. Often we find ourselves busy with the cares of life, the responsibilities of jobs, deadlines, and bills. And our children will invite us into a simple moment of magic to pause, play with a ball, or sit next to a flowing creek. These shared moments will become the memories we cherish most as we look back on the story of our family. These are the experiences that fill our future table.

THE GIFT OF RELATIONSHIP

JENNI

Practicing awe opens our eyes to see those around us as a gift to cherish rather than a burden to bear. Relationships are hard, yes. Marriage, parenting, and friendships all require hard work. But we can't live from that mindset. If I set up camp in the perspective that shows me only all that's difficult about what I am walking through, I will find no strength there.

When I choose instead to see my days and my relationships as an incredible gift, and I search for specific things to offer thanks for, even in the difficult parts, it's there I find the strength, grace, and hope I need to keep loving others well. I love what pastor Tyler Staton says: "There is no better response to a gift giver than to enjoy the gift, and there is no sweeter worship to God than to enjoy the life that he has given you to live."[4] Practicing awe shifts our perspective from merely surviving each day to seeing life as the great gift from the Lord that it truly is. What I have found is that when I make a regular practice of pausing to take in the glimpses of awe all around me, it's like making a deposit into my awe tank, and when difficult times come, as they always do, I then have a sizable amount of awe to draw from.

Shifting our eyes to see this rhythm of home we're crafting as a gift to cherish can pull us almost immediately into a better place. Each day, if I let it, this practice of awe can change the way I see. It reminds me what a privilege it is to be alive. It turns ordinary, small things into holy things. What a privilege to have a family, to journey through this incredible adventure called life together. Not only do I get to live this life, but I get to walk through it with this incredible guy standing next to me. A man who loves me and makes me feel beautiful every day. I get to live down the hall from these five beautiful blond babes. I get to be stretched and challenged and honored and loved by them every day. As Thomas Howard put it, "Holy things are ordinary things perceived in their true light, that is, as bearers of the divine mysteries and glory to us."[5]

There are moments that come to us unbidden, opportunities to lean into the awe of the world as we know it right now, in this season. Chris is so good at seeing these moments and slowing to take them in. I, too, am learning how to pause to participate in the simple delight of the moment. I'm learning that practicing awe requires keeping our eyes open to the beauty and wonder hidden throughout our days. Training our eyes to see each day as a gift, one that we don't get to enjoy if we're too busy to unwrap it. If we merely survive it. Skim through it. Enjoying the gift of relationship involves looking for gratitude in the middle of the ordinary.

EYES OF AWE

I've always had an overly expressive face. I'm not kidding. Growing up, it was a running joke among my family and friends. There's no hiding how I'm feeling at any given moment. Apparently, it's written all over my face. These expressions of mine have been known to stop professors mid-lecture, youth pastors mid-sermon, and even an artist mid-concert to ask me in front of the entire class/youth group/audience, "Jenni/Hey you/Girl in the third row, what in the world are you thinking? You just have to explain that look on your face."

The looks we give hold incredible power. A single look can speak a thousand words. I have often learned the hard way that how I choose to look toward my kids *truly* matters. It impacts them for better or worse, whether I intend it to or not. My face communicates how I feel toward them and even what kind of people I believe them to be.

"[Kids] look at our face like a mirror. What are we saying with our face? Are we saying, 'You bother me; I'm tolerating you'? . . . When you realize that God's actually leaning into [the] relationship that He has with us, then as parents we get that same privilege of reflecting back to our kids, 'No, I delight in you,'" notes Jan Foreman.[6] We gauge our beliefs about ourselves by the way the important people in our lives see us. When the most important people in kids' lives, their parents, see them as a beautiful gift, something within them starts to shift, and they begin to act like one. We have the opportunity to reflect God's love to our kids through the way we choose to delight in them.

Just like the words we speak over each other, the way we look at our kids—especially over time—can affect who they become. The rhythm of awe is powerful because it gives us a new lens through which to see our family. As we begin to see our spouse with eyes of awe and gratitude, our actions—and even feelings—more easily follow. Reminding myself of the great gift my kids are to me empowers me to extend more compassion during conflict, lean into their lives with fresh curiosity, and see the beauty and blessings they carry. Practicing awe toward them allows me to receive all that they have to give.

So what do we do when conflict arises with our children? When their behavior causes us to feel the opposite of awe toward them? How do we shift our hearts to see them through eyes of awe and gratitude then? The most helpful tool I have found to shift my perspective in the moment is to remember the best, most lovable version of my kid and choose to see that person instead. I have also learned that if for some reason the behavior has affected me so much that I cannot find that better, truer version of them in the moment, it's really important that I walk away and take a breather until I can get my emotions under control and gain a better perspective. A look can say a thousand words.

Do whatever you can to shift your perspective in the heat of the moment. This reminds your kids how much you love them (because they can actually see it in your eyes) and who they truly are (because they can also see that person reflected in your eyes)—and it empowers you to remember the same. You are choosing to believe the best of them, rather than believing the behavior they may be exhibiting in the moment. Family therapist Jennifer Kolari advises,

> Find a way to think about your child at their best. You have to center yourself, and *that's* where you need to be in your mind. . . . If you are responding to your child and you look terrified of them . . . they're going to look at you, gauge that response, and think, "Oh my gosh, I really *am* that scary. I really *am* that big of a mess."[7]

Make a consistent, intentional practice of looking in awe at your kids—as they walk into the room, as they step onto the court, as they stroll up to the car in the pickup line. In the younger years, you may find them returning your gaze with equal excitement and delight. As they enter the tumultuous teen years, they may roll an eye, but nevertheless, parent, press on! Do it anyway. They are being shaped, very much indeed, by the depth of awe (or lack of awe) they see in our eyes.

PRACTICING THE RHYTHM

As a concept, awe might feel distant and inaccessible, but the reality is that there are countless opportunities to practice staying in awe every day. So how do we practice living in awe in the middle of our ordinary lives? How can we intentionally approach each other with eyes of curiosity, gratitude, and wonder? Here are some thoughts to get you started.

Watch for This-Is-It Moments

One of our favorite family sayings is *This is it*. I can't remember the first time Chris said those words, but over time they've become a consistent way to mark the golden moments of our family life. We'll be snuggled up by the fire, watching the kids roast their marshmallows and hearing them tell their stories, and Chris will lean over to me and say, "This is it. Right here. It just doesn't get any better than this."

We know those bright moments won't last forever. The rain will come, the kids will find something to argue about, and life will move on. But as we pause to acknowledge the magic, to catch and name those glimpses of awe, we create joy together. In fact, as a therapist friend of ours recently reminded us, when we intentionally chose awe in a moment of celebration, our joy doubles. As philosopher G. K. Chesterton put it, "Gratitude is happiness doubled by wonder."[8]

When you find yourself in a moment that stirs your soul, *lean into it*. Reveling in the sacredness of life, even in the fleeting pieces of our days, keeps our faith awake and our souls alive.

Practice Gratitude

When we find ourselves in a dry season and awe is hard to come by, gratitude is what restores and revives us. And I'm not talking about having a vague positive thought or willing ourselves to be thankful. Gratitude takes intention. It requires paying attention and choosing to give thanks, even in the smallest things. There is always something to be grateful for.

As I walked around the neighborhood this afternoon, the snap of a trash can made me look up. A young boy, maybe eleven or twelve, was taking the trash out for his family. He reminded me so much of our oldest at that age—so sweet and helpful, kind and good-hearted. Our son is nearly eighteen now, and the days with him under our roof are numbered. I can't go anywhere these days without being reminded. And there it was again, a wave of emotion coming for me.

In that moment, I sensed the choices in front of me. I could wallow in the grief I felt rising. I could ignore it, avoid it, and distract myself from feeling any of it. Or I could allow the grief and joy to exist together. I could look for the awe hidden within the love and gratitude I feel for our extraordinary son and the time we've had with him here.

So as I turned the corner for home, I let the tears flow as they needed to and then offered up a silent thanks. For the gift of this sweet season of life, where all five beloved blond heads of ours have lived just down the hall. For the unbelievable privilege it is to be their mom. I closed my eyes, lifted my head, and whispered, "Thank you, Lord. Thank you for the beautiful season we've had together as a family all these years, and for the beautiful new season you're leading us into." And I felt the rush of joy on the other side of grief. Practicing awe for this great gift of being his mom brought me back to the joy that is always there too, right under the surface of grief. If we pause to look for it and to offer thanks for it, we'll find ourselves increasingly living in a posture of awe.

Here are some other everyday ideas to practice gratitude and awe:

- Keep a folder on your phone or an album by your bed of the connections that carry you. Remembering to be grateful for those relationships is one of our greatest defenses against discouragement.

- Create an "awe wall." I put up a huge pinboard on the wall next to my nightstand and filled it with inspiring images that stir my soul, sweet snapshots of awe-filled moments with friends and family, kind notes from my kids, and encouraging cards from caring friends. Every morning and night, I'm reminded of the goodness around me, and I'm propelled again into awe and wonder.
- Create a playlist of songs that stir your soul and remind you of what's beautiful and true. (See the playlist at www .therhythmofus.com for inspiration.)
- Tape a meaningful verse—something that points you back to God's truth about the gift of family—to your dash or mirror or set it as the screen saver on your phone, where you will see it daily.

Set the Scene for Wonder

When our kids turn twelve, they each get to take a trip with me, just the two of us. We do this to savor that last, delicious year of childhood before they officially become teenagers and to allow time for those important conversations to happen that seem to only occur as we slow down and savor time together.

We also try to intentionally make space for awe and wonder along the way, both in planning meaningful experiences of beauty and in praying for eyes to see the unexpected moments of awe that invite us in along the way. It's an amazing experience to set aside time when the only agenda is delight, connection, and awe. I highly recommend it.

Other everyday ideas to set the scene for awe:

- Plan a family campout under the stars. (S'mores are a helpful addition.)
- Go for a family awe walk or hike together on the prettiest trails you can find.
- Light a fire and gather your people around it. There's something magical about sitting around the fire together. Somehow it seems to pull conversations out of us like no other setting can.

We can choose to pause and lean into moments of awe as they come to us, but we can also plan for experiences that set us up for it. Seek experiences of awe as a family.

Pray

One of the habits we love to practice with our kids at bedtime is the Prayer of Examen. Journeying together through the events of the day helps us pause to notice moments to be grateful for and where the magic was hidden throughout the day.

To go through the Prayer of Examen together as a family, start by reflecting on the day's events. If you have a visual kid, drawing or writing it all out in a journal can be really helpful. Begin with gratitude, looking for the ordinary moments where you can point your kids toward a posture of thankfulness. Then ask them to list the moments they remember from the day. Help them pinpoint emotions they felt along the way. Our older kids can name their emotions. For our younger ones, I have them draw a face next to each piece of the day, expressing how they felt in the moment. Talk through each feeling. Look for opportunities to highlight where God might be working, to acknowledge a child's strengths, or to rewrite the story. Close by asking, "What could the Lord be trying to show us today? What can we learn from today to take with us into tomorrow?"

I can't stress enough the power of prayer. Find a way to pray that works for you, and commit to it consistently. Chris loves to pray out loud, so good times for him are before the kids wake up and when he's alone in the car. I love to journal, so before bed, I like to write out prayers for each kid. There's usually a worry or two to lay at the Lord's feet, and I'll write those out in a prayer of surrender.

Our kids will never outgrow the need for our prayers. The greatest way we can bless them is by covering their lives with intentional prayer.

CHOOSING AWE IN THE HARD MOMENTS

Practicing this rhythm of awe in the golden moments, when it comes naturally, is one thing. It's easy to find overwhelming gratitude when you're walking hand in hand with your child as the sun sets, pausing to let the beautiful moment wash over you and strengthen your soul. But what about the rest of life? What about the hard moments we all experience as parents? Where the sacredness of parenting is covered up by the most difficult parts? We all experience them. It's just part of life. Where is awe to be found then?

Lately the Lord has been teaching me that it's actually amid these most difficult moments, when finding awe and gratitude is the last thing we feel like doing, that the practice of awe can offer us the most strength and peace. The power of this rhythm is found not only in pausing to practice awe in the beautiful moments where it comes easily but also by looking for awe in the difficult times. He's leading me to see ways to offer gratitude in the hard places . . . and the peace that is found on the other side.

It happened to me just a few months ago as I was driving home from a trip to the mall with my teenage daughter. If you have entered the teen years at all with your kiddos, you will likely relate to this story. The early teen years can feel so foreign. Life as an adolescent is not easy, and neither is parenting them through it. It's the beginning of them having to walk through real-life struggles, and of us not being able to step in and fix their problems for them. They have to find their own way through, and we have to let them.

As a friend recently reminded us, "All those prayers we've prayed for them since they were born—that they'll be brave, that they'll become strong, that they will change their world for the better—they can't become *any* of those things if they never have to walk through hard things. They are shaped by these hard days."

As parents, the hardest thing in the world is to watch the child you love more than anything have to struggle through real trials. But as we remember that this is how they become the strong, brave, incredible humans God has called them to be, we can trust Him with the story He's writing for them. We can get on our knees a little more, and if we're willing, we can let the experience grow us into stronger, braver humans as well.

Adolescence is also the beginning of letting go. It's *never* easy. Suddenly, the kid whose greatest wish was to be constantly by your side is now begging you to drop them off three blocks from their destination so they don't have to be seen with you!

The child who used to ask your advice about everything is now rolling his eyes at any input you offer. What wise parenting sages who have gone before us have assured us is: *They do come back.* Now, listen, I understand. It can feel almost cruel to see that so casually written while you're in the middle of the adolescent-angst phase. But I can tell you even now, with our oldest teens at fifteen and almost eighteen, that it really is true. Everyone has to walk through the tunnel of adolescence. But when our kids come through on the other side, they really are wonderful again—stronger, even! Practice staying in awe of the great gift it is to be your child's parent, even in the hard places. Keep on loving, keep on looking for the good, keep on choosing *them*. They do come back. They really do.

I remember the exact moment God began teaching me this practice of choosing awe in the hard times. We were in what felt like the height of the adolescent angst with our teenage daughter, who was walking through all manner of those "character building" struggles we mentioned before. She has become a stronger, more courageous human because of walking through that season, but while she was in the midst of it, we were all struggling to find our way through. She has graciously allowed me to share this moment with you while also offering you encouragement as a teen who's been through it: "It gets better, I promise!"

The mall is my least favorite place to be, but I chose to go because I love my daughter and was hoping that by entering her world I would at least get some good conversation time on the drive there and back. Things did not go according to plan. No matter what questions I asked, one-word responses were all she seemed able to respond with.

As we drove home in silence, I offered up a quiet prayer to the Lord. *God, I need your help here. I'm trying. I'm doing everything I can, and I don't see any evidence of it working. I just miss her. I miss the preadolescent friendship we used to share. I need your help here.*

What began to stir in my spirit I know was from the Lord because I had never thought of it before: "Practice awe right now." *Right now?* I thought. *Really?* I looked over my shoulder to see if there was a rainbow or sunset I had missed. *Where is the wonder?* I thought. *Where is the beauty?* But as I let the idea turn over in my head, I began to see. The truth is, it's in these very moments—when it's just *hard,* when the response you want is not happening, when you're walking with your child through a tough season—where the practice of awe can revive us most. As John Eldredge puts it, "Beauty rescues. . . . Beauty heals, partly because it proclaims that there is goodness in the world and that goodness prevails."[9]

He was right. I can practice awe even in the middle of the hard moments. I can choose to remember that this parenting thing is all a great gift, even the difficult parts, and receive the joy and peace that comes on the other side of it.

So as we came to a red light, I closed my eyes, took a deep breath, and exhaled a silent thank-you for this great gift of *her.* For the beautiful blessing of our life together and for the unbelievable privilege it is to be her mom. Even on the hard days, I wouldn't trade it for the world. She's one of the most amazing people I know, and I love her so much. *Thank you, Lord.*

And there it was, that peace. The kind that passes all understanding. The kind that guards our hearts and minds in Christ Jesus (Philippians 4:7). There it was.

In *every* situation, give thanks. Practice gratitude. For all God has done, for all He is doing, and for all that He is planning to do. Even when I can't see it, God is up to something good. In every season, He provides a way for us to find awe, to offer our gratitude, to trust Him with the story He's writing. Keep looking for awe. It's there. It's always there.

May we become the kind of people who look for the beauty around us and point it out to others, especially to the little ones looking up to us. Who give thanks for each moment to the Giver of all good gifts. And may we become the kind of parents who treat our kids as the remarkable gifts they truly are and who remember the incredible value of the life we've been given to live together. *This is it.*

PRACTICE

- What have been your richest experiences of awe?

- Start a gratitude journal of things you notice about your kids.

- Send your kids a quick text every morning or evening with just one thing you're thankful for about them. Or leave a note on their door!

- Pray for eyes to see the magic hidden in the mundane. Make it a goal to find at least one moment of awe every day.

PART THREE

UNIQUE FAMILY RHYTHMS

AS WE DISCUSSED in the beginning of the book, finding our rhythm as a family takes a lot of time, a lot of trial and error, and a lot of leaning on the Lord to guide us. But whether we realize it or not, we already have a "rhythm of home," a set of regular habits that are forming our family culture and shaping who we are becoming along the way. The question is, do we like where our rhythm is taking us? In other words, do we like the kind of family our habits are leading us to become?

The truth is, the rhythms we live from today will determine who we become tomorrow.

More than likely, your family already has a set of rhythms that carry you through your days. In this section we will move toward greater awareness of those family rhythms by taking the time to notice and name each one, then evaluate its place in your family life. Recognizing the rhythms that bring us joy and move us toward the life we long to create enables us to see their value and propels us to prioritize them.

As you reflect on the habits that fill your home, you may run across at least a handful of rhythms that have begun to feel more like ruts. Taking the time to recognize and remove these obstacles is an important part of filling your days with the rhythms that bring you the most life.

Reflect on your life as a family over the last few days, weeks, and months, and observe the rhythms that bring you the most joy, life, and closeness, the habits that naturally cause your heart to feel alive—and those that consistently drain you. Building your rhythm of home is a powerful way to pour intentionality into the habits you value most, moving your family step by step toward the life you long to create.

9

FAMILY HABITS INVENTORY

Examining Your Household Rhythms

WHICH RHYTHMS FLOW from our deepest values? Which habits pull us away from those values? We can take an honest look at the habits we practice together as well as our individual habits that affect the family.

Be as honest and specific as you can, remembering that all change begins with honesty. Resist the urge to point fingers or shame anyone's habits. This is never helpful. Create a shame-free space where everyone can share. Take a true inventory of the practices that fill your days.

PERSONAL RHYTHMS INVENTORY

Describe a "day in the life" for you.

....
....
....
....
....
....

Which rhythms bring you joy?

....
....
....
....
....
....

Are there any activities you find particularly draining?

....
....
....
....
....
....

Which activities lift your spirits and make you feel at home?

....

....

....

....

....

Which rhythms move you toward the person you want to become?

....

....

....

....

....

Which rhythms pull you away from the person you want to become?

....

....

....

....

....

Which rhythms stir your heart for God?

....

....

....

....

Which habits distract you or pull you away from your relationship with God?

....

....

....

....

....

....

Are there any rhythms that almost work but could be improved in some way?

....

....

....

....

....

....

Are there any activities missing from your day that you'd like to create space for?

....

....

....

....

....

....

FAMILY RHYTHMS INVENTORY

Which rhythms create a sense of closeness as a family?

....

....

....

....

Which rhythms align most with your highest family values?

....

....

....

....

Which habits distract you from your highest family values?

....

....

....

....

Which rhythms are already working well for you or bring you joy? Why?

....

....

....

....

Which habits cause consistent conflict or friction?

....
....
....
....
....

Which habits pull you away from each other?

....
....
....
....
....

Which rhythms are your favorites?

....
....
....
....

Which rhythms no longer fit the life you want to move toward as a family?

....
....
....
....

Are there any activities missing from your day that you should create space for? What would need to shift for that to happen?

....

....

....

....

....

If you could choose anywhere to get away as a family together, where would it be and what would you do?

....

....

....

....

Which rhythms or ruts move you away from the family culture you desire?

....

....

....

....

Which rhythms draw you closer to God as a family?

....

....

....

....

What are some ways you can proactively say yes to each other throughout the week?

....

....

....

....

....

Which rhythms in your family life leave you feeling the most hurried, both individually and collectively?

....

....

....

....

....

PULLING IT ALL TOGETHER

Rhythms worth prioritizing:

....

....

....

....

....

Rhythms worth keeping and improving:

....

....

....

....

....

Rhythms worth letting go of to make space for what truly matters:

....

....

....

....

....

10

FAMILY VALUES INVENTORY

Evaluating Your Top Core Values

OUR RHYTHMS EMERGE out of what we value. That's why when the rhythms that fill our days together flow from our deepest shared values, we experience the thriving family culture we long for. Use this inventory to help uncover what matters most to you, both individually and as a family.

Discuss what makes each of you come alive, what stirs your soul and brings you the most joy. Each person matters; everyone gets a voice. Name any important values you may have drifted from somewhere along the way.

Give each person permission to honestly name the things

that matter most to them. There is a lot of power in leaning in to really listen to what someone else cares about. Create a safe, judgment-free space for your family to share what matters and any areas of family life that may be causing conflict or pain. Help your kids discover what value that could be pointing to. Write it down. Connect with other thriving families in your circle of friends. Invite them over for dinner, and ask what their highest priorities are as a family. What things do they refuse to allow in their home? Write it all down here. Be as specific and honest as you can. Writing things down helps signal to our brains to pay attention to and remember things we value.[1] Don't worry about getting it perfect or final—this is just about naming what matters most to you and your family.

WHAT MATTERS MOST

What activities make you come alive personally?

....

....

....

....

What activities make you come alive as a family?

....

....

....

....

What do you hope to be known for as a family?

....

....

....

....

Are there any important values you feel like your family may have drifted from?

....

....

....

....

Are there any areas of your life together that consistently bring joy? What value could the joy be pointing to?

....

....

....

....

What areas of your life continually cause conflict or stress? What value could they be pointing to?

....

....

....

....

Name a family who inspires you. What are some of their values?

....

....

....

....

....

In the middle portion of this book, we identified five healthy rhythms, each of which emerges from specific values. We *speak life* because we value the power of words. We *serve* because we value caring for others. We *slow down* because we value meaningful connection. We *seek adventure* because we value growth and life-changing experiences. We *stay in awe* because we value seeing life as a beautiful gift.

With that in mind, reflect on the rhythms you've identified as key to your family culture, and take a moment to identify the values they reflect. Underneath each value, brainstorm a few intentional ways you could integrate touchpoints of these values into your everyday life as a family.

For example, if you listed the value of *health*, your practices might include things like these:

- Shoot hoops together as a family on Tuesdays and Thursdays after dinner.
- Look up healthy recipes and choose a handful to try this month.
- Create a chart on the fridge to log each person's daily veggie intake. The winner picks a prize.

Value:

Practices:

Value:

Practices:

Value:

Practices:

Remember, there are a thousand different ways we could choose to create and live into our family culture. We move toward the thriving family we long to be when we intentionally center our lives on the values and rhythms that lead us toward God and each other.

11

FAMILY VISION INVENTORY

Naming the Life You Envision

AT THE BEGINNING OF THIS JOURNEY, you spent some time dreaming about your future family culture—the hopes and dreams you and your family have for your relationships and legacy. Now that you've explored the core rhythms and thought through some of your current habits and values, it's time to discuss what those visions look like. Vision is seeing into the future before it exists, and the more you can keep that vision in front of you, the stronger your family culture can become.

Naming your individual visions for your life together (and

yes, that includes your kids!) and seeing where they align and differ allows you to be on the same page so you can work together to move toward where you want to go. It also allows you to identify the areas of your life that are already in wonderful alignment with or close to that vision and to assess where you may need some work.

Take some time to envision and put into words the life you want to create together. What does your family life look like in your wildest dreams? Maybe you've done this before, when you began your family, but it's been a while and your vision has changed. Or maybe you've never actually put words to the life you want. Now is your time. Maybe it looks like carving out more consistent nights to spend together as a family or opening up your home to fill it with good people, being intentional with the village you're cultivating. What type of home do you dream of living in? What do you hope people feel when they enter it? What places do you dream of going as a family? Write it all down. We have found it helpful to start by mapping out our dream together as a couple, then including the kids.

After you've clearly named your vision, set aside some time to talk through the future you desire. Make it special. It doesn't have to be fancy—just intentional. Light some candles, put on a good playlist, make a favorite meal or dessert, and then talk through what your life together looks like in your wildest dreams. Everyone gets a say. Everyone's voice matters.

What does your family culture look like in your wildest dreams?

....

....

....

....

What do you want to be true of you as a family? What do you hope will be said of you?

....

....

....

....

When you celebrate each kid on their graduation day, what do you hope will be on that table?

....

....

....

....

As you discuss your individual ideas for the future, what areas are alike?

....

....

....

....

What areas are different?

....

....

....

....

....

Which aspects of your vision are already part of your life?

....

....

....

....

....

Which parts of the vision are most important in this current season?
What are some things you could work on together to make them
a reality?

....

....

....

....

....

....

12

PUTTING IT ALL TOGETHER

Your Rhythm of Home

⊕HIS IS THE FUN PART of the journey, where all the reflecting, uncovering, and dreaming comes together to encompass your unique rhythm of home, your pathway toward a thriving family culture. Glance back at your list of rhythms to keep, your core values, and your vision of the future. What surfaced as your family considered each question? Did anything surprise you? What areas of your vision were different from your spouse's or your children's? What areas were the same?

Maybe you found that you're closer to your vision than

you thought, or at least headed in the right direction. Maybe you found yourself stuck in ruts you don't want. Now is the time to get unstuck. Prioritize the values of the rhythms over the details.

With time and practice, each of these rhythms can start to become part of the natural flow of life together. It's important to intentionally make space for each value by putting it on the calendar and by looking for opportunities to practice it.

Here we've provided some ideas to get you started as you think through different rhythms that work for you and your family. Each of the core rhythms is included, and there's space for you to include the unique rhythms you've identified as well.

SPEAKING LIFE

- *Think of one positive thing about each family member, then take a moment to acknowledge it out loud around the dinner table.*

-

-

-

SERVING

- Sneak a bag filled with your kid's favorite treats into their locker on the day of a big test, audition, or game.

-

-

-

SLOWING DOWN

- Which activities have your children been consistently inviting you to join them in? Surprise them this week by making it happen. Maybe it's building a fort together in the middle of the living room, whisking them away for a family campout underneath the stars, or picking them up early from school to grab their favorite drink and go for a drive together.

-

-

-

SEEKING ADVENTURE

- Discover something your child's been dreaming of doing. Find at least one way to water that dream by helping them bring it to life.

-

-

-

STAYING IN AWE

- Find the power-off button on your phone, grab your family, and head to the prettiest trails you can find. As you walk together, take in the beauty of God's creation all around you. Take a deep breath, and smell the fresh scents of nature around you. As you walk, notice how it lifts your mood, eases your worries, and draws you closer to one another.

-

-

-

UNIQUE RHYTHM: ....

-

-

-

UNIQUE RHYTHM: ....

-

-

-

UNIQUE RHYTHM: ....

-

-

-

Do It Anyway

Grace for the Journey

Light is sweet; how pleasant to see a new day dawning.
ECCLESIASTES 11:7, NLT

LIFE WILL THROW YOU CURVEBALLS. Always. There will be millions of ups and downs and twists and turns along the way. When it's all said and done, family life will look like all different types of days. Some days the kids will respond with joy and gratitude to the intentional rhythms you work to create. Other days they will seem to barely notice or will even balk at your efforts to cultivate a rich, loving family culture. Remember our mantra: *Do it anyway*. As a mentor recently reminded us, "Your faithfulness to God's ways is not contingent on others' responses toward you. Your obedience to Him has nothing to do with their reaction. You be faithful." You do it anyway.

As we choose to follow the Lord's leading, step by step, choice by choice, we are headed somewhere *good*. Rain will come, plans will go awry, and hot chocolate will spill. Do it anyway. There is *so much more* growing beneath the surface that we simply cannot see. Don't give up, friend. The harvest is coming. And it will take your breath away.

AS YOU GO

Speak Life to Yourself

Consider the daily thoughts that are fueling your actions. Are they speaking life or death? Guard against any beliefs that may be hindering your progress. Do you believe God is with you, even in the tough moments? Do you believe He has good things planned for you and your family? Do you believe He is strong enough to bring healing to your family where it is needed? Notice and name any lies that may be creeping in, and replace them with the truth of God's Word.

Lean into Your Village

Ask God to surround you with other thriving families. Invest time and energy into cultivating those relationships. We cannot stress this enough. If we are attempting to practice healthy rhythms while we're surrounded by influences that lead us in the opposite direction, our efforts will often be in vain. Watch the company you keep. We simply cannot build a thriving family alone. God wisely wired us to need both Him and each other. Seek out parents around you who are following God's ways for raising their families, and lean into them.

Review

Keep coming back to the rhythm of home you created for your family, to review and reassess. Find a spot in your home where you can all be reminded daily of the vision you're after. Create a vision board representing each rhythm, fill up a felt letter board outlining each practice, or encourage your kids to write a song about it. Get creative and involve your family. They will be more motivated to practice your family rhythms if you involve them in the process of creating and celebrating them.

It's also important to review your rhythm of home as the seasons of your family life shift. Make sure your rhythms are serving you and your family, not the other way around. Just as you and your family are changing and growing along the way, so will the ways in which you can intentionally live out your highest values. Review your rhythms from time to time, and tweak as needed.

Pray

Soak each day in prayer. One of my favorite summer camps as a kid, with the most beautiful environment, had this one thing that set it apart: The leaders prayed over *everything*. Not just meals and services—I mean *everything*. If you signed up for horseback riding or crafting or bike riding, it would always begin and end with prayer. If you asked to talk with one of the counselors, you could bet on hearing, "Can we start with prayer?" Whatever the activity, the starting point was set: *prayer*. And you could feel the difference in the air. The atmosphere that the counselors cultivated was rich and welcoming because they made a regular rhythm of inviting the Lord in.

Pray over everything you can. Nothing will shift the

atmosphere of our homes like a regular rhythm of prayer. Invite the Lord into every moment, both silently within your own heart and out loud in front of your kids. Road trips, soccer games, craft times, mealtimes, bedtimes—what if you began each one with prayer? Give it a try.

A BLESSING
FOR THE JOURNEY

> If ever there was a school of love, it is the family.
> WENDY WRIGHT

So, FRIENDS, AS YOU CLOSE THIS BOOK and begin your journey toward the thriving family life you long for, whether you are just beginning your family or are farther down the road, may you always remember you are never alone. God is with you. You have what it takes. He's always been with you, and He always will be.

May you pay attention to the moments that seem to stop time and trust the story God is writing for you and for your precious family. May you lean into your village, invite God's grace

into the hard moments, and speak life over the beautiful lives
He's given you to shape. May you serve each other with all your
hearts, slow down to savor each moment you have together, and
say yes to each adventure the Lord invites you into along the
way! And above all, may you stay wildly in awe of the great gift
it is to be a family.

Here's to the wonder of family.
Here's to grace and strength for your beautiful journey.
Here's to *the rhythm of home*.

Also by Chris and Jenni Graebe

Discover the Five Rhythms of a Thriving Marriage

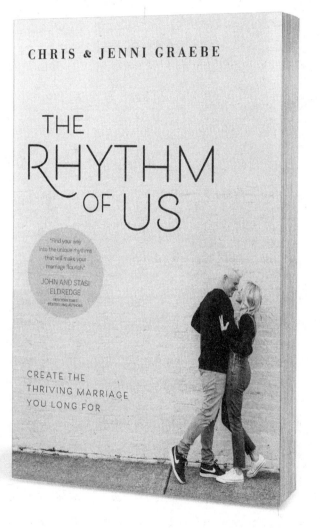

CP1975

JOURNALING PAGES

ACKNOWLEDGMENTS

LOVE AND THANKS to our wonderful families, the Heflins and the Graebes. We are so blessed to call you ours!

This project came to be not in regular daily rhythms of writing (as we would have chosen) but rather in fits and starts. In early mornings and late nights. In stolen hours here and there. And in a few long, glorious weekends, spent mostly surrounded by the beautiful trees at The Brooks at Weatherford (Texas) and Bear Creek, Tennessee. We are so grateful to my (Jenni's) parents, Steve and Tricia, for so generously offering these breathtaking settings for us to enjoy a quiet place to put pen to paper. You have always been the ultimate example of love and generosity to us. Thank you doesn't come close to cutting it for the gift that you both are in our lives. We love you so much!

Thanks and love to my mom, Tricia, for the million hours spent watching your granddaughters so this book could become a reality. They are all better for time spent with Grammie! We're so thankful for you!

A thousand thanks to our wonderful editors, Caitlyn and Dave, for believing so much in this message and for asking the right questions to make this project better. We are forever grateful. To our copy editor Elizabeth: Your insights and attention to detail are always a blessing! To the entire team at NavPress and Tyndale House Publishers: We are forever grateful for the honor of partnering with you to make much of Jesus and His incredible design for families!

Thank you to our dear friend and gifted photographer, Meshali Mitchell, for using your amazing gift to capture such a beautiful cover shot. You are the best!

Thank you to our wonderful friends and mentors who encouraged us and faithfully cheered us on along this journey of bringing a book to life! We have learned so much from you—thank you for teaching us well! Special thanks to John and Stasi Eldredge, Mark and Jan Foreman, Michael and Linda Adler, Christy Nockles, Jeannie Cunnion, and Angie Smith. Your advice, prayers, and support have been the greatest gift.

Lastly, all our love to our phenomenal kids: Kaden, Addie, Averi, Kennedi, and Keris. You are the absolute light of our lives. Being your mom and dad is our very favorite thing we get to do. Thank you for filling our lives with so much awe and wonder. You are our greatest adventure!

NOTES

INTRODUCTION: THE SACRED JOURNEY OF PARENTING

1. Wendy M. Wright, *Seasons of a Family's Life* (San Francisco: Jossey-Bass, 2003), 18.
2. See Chris and Jenni Graebe, *The Rhythm of Us* (Colorado Springs: NavPress, 2021). We could get almost everything else wrong in life and in parenting, but if our kids know deep down that Mom and Dad love each other, we're providing them with the greatest gift possible. Start with your marriage.
3. Margaret Guenther, *At Home in the World* (New York: Seabury Books, 2006), 13.

1: BUILDING YOUR FAMILY TABLE

1. Dr. Henry Cloud, "The Importance of Having a Vision," Boundaries course, https://www.boundaries.me.
2. Thomas Howard, *Hallowed Be This House*, rev. ed. (San Francisco: Ignatius Press, 2012), 25.
3. Mark and Jan Foreman, *Never Say No* (Colorado Springs: David C Cook, 2015), 89.
4. D. Ross Campbell, *How to Really Love Your Child*, 3rd ed. (Colorado Springs: David C Cook, 2015), 72–73.

2: WARMTH WITHIN THE WALLS

1. Maya Angelou, *All God's Children Need Traveling Shoes* (New York: Vintage Books, 1991), 196.
2. Andi Ashworth, *Real Love for Real Life* (Colorado Springs: WaterBrook, 2002), 60.

3. Wendell Berry, *Hannah Coulter* (Washington, DC: Shoemaker & Hoard, 2004), 83.

4. Ashworth, *Real Love for Real Life*, 55.

5. Mark and Jan Foreman interview with Natalie Stilwell, "Raising Creative Kids," So Goes the Future, June 24, 2021, YouTube video, https://www.youtube.com/watch?v=MkNqflcn3fg.

6. John Eldredge interview with Chris and Jenni Graebe, "72. John Eldredge: Get Your Life Back," *The Rhythm of Us* (podcast), February 25, 2020, https://www.therhythmofus.com/podcasts/the-rhythm-of-us/episodes/2147808895.

7. Fred Rogers, *Many Ways to Say I Love You*, rev. ed. (New York: Hachette Books, 2019), foreword.

3: IT TAKES A VILLAGE

1. Just in case anyone missed this, these are lyrics from the classic '90s youth group song "Thank You" by Ray Boltz (from his 1988 album *Thank You*).

2. Jim Rohn, quoted in Aimee Groth, "You're the Average of the Five People You Spend the Most Time With," Business Insider, July 24, 2012, https://www.businessinsider.com/jim-rohn-youre-the-average-of-the-five-people-you-spend-the-most-time-with-2012-7.

3. John O'Donohue, *To Bless the Space between Us* (New York: Doubleday, 2008), 213.

4. Albert Schweitzer, *Memoirs of Childhood and Youth* (London: Allen & Unwin, 1924), 90.

5. As quoted in Leonard Sweet, *Nudge* (Colorado Springs: David C Cook, 2010), 52.

6. Christy Nockels, "Keep On," *This Is the Hour*, Keepers Branch Records, 2023.

4: *GRACE* IS THE WORD

1. This quote seems to be generally attributed to Michael Nolan. See https://www.goodreads.com/author/quotes/136408.Michael_Nolan.

2. John O'Donohue, *To Bless the Space between Us* (New York: Doubleday, 2008), 217.

3. O'Donohue, *To Bless the Space between Us*, 186.

4. O'Donohue, *To Bless the Space between Us*, 198–199.

5. O'Donohue, *To Bless the Space between Us*, 198.

5: MY LIFE FOR YOURS

1. Thomas Howard, *Hallowed Be This House*, rev. ed. (San Francisco: Ignatius Press, 2012), 50.

2. Dr. Henry Cloud, "The Importance of Having a Vision," Boundaries course, https://www.boundaries.me.

3. Andi Ashworth, *Real Love for Real Life* (Colorado Springs: WaterBrook, 2002), 69.

6: SAYING YES

1. Mark and Jan Foreman, *Never Say No* (Colorado Springs: David C Cook, 2015), 13.

2. D. Ross Campbell, *How to Really Love Your Child*, 3rd ed. (Colorado Springs: David C Cook, 2015), 71.

3. Mark Foreman, "Parenting While Pastoring," The Resolved Church, October 3, 2018, YouTube video, https://www.youtube.com/watch?v=nyI2oklb1Fc.

4. Blue Letter Bible, "Lexicon: Strong's G1949—*epilambanomai*," accessed July 13, 2023, https://www.blueletterbible.org/lexicon/g1949/kjv/tr/0-1.

5. Blue Letter Bible, "Lexicon: Strong's G2222—*zōē*," accessed July 13, 2023, https://www.blueletterbible.org/lexicon/g2222/kjv/tr/0-1.

7: LIFE ON THE EDGE

1. Eugene H. Peterson, *Run with the Horses*, commem. ed. (Downers Grove, IL: InterVarsity Press, 2019), 148.

2. Eugene H. Peterson, *The Contemplative Pastor* (Grand Rapids, MI: Eerdmans, 1993), 72.

3. Harold Wood, "Saint John Muir," Sierra Club (website), updated April 17, 2019, https://vault.sierraclub.org/john_muir_exhibit/life/saint_john_muir.aspx.

4. Eugene H. Peterson, *The Wisdom of Each Other* (Grand Rapids, MI: Zondervan, 1998), 9–10.

5. Margaret Guenther, *At Home in the World* (New York: Seabury Books, 2006), 120.

6. John O'Donohue, *To Bless the Space between Us* (New York: Doubleday, 2008), 192.

7. John Eldredge, *Wild at Heart*, rev. and expanded (Nashville: Thomas Nelson, 2010). Eldredge explores what he calls the "core question" of men throughout the book.

8: THIS IS IT

1. Howard Thurman, "The Singing of Angels," in *For the Inward Journey* (Richmond, IN: Friends United Press, 1984), 247.

2. John O'Donohue, *To Bless the Space between Us* (New York: Doubleday, 2008), 190.

3. Paul David Tripp, *Awe* (Wheaton, IL: Crossway, 2015), 20.

4. Tyler Staton, Ash Wednesday service, Oaks Church Brooklyn, February 17, 2021.

5. Thomas Howard, *Hallowed Be This House*, rev. ed. (San Francisco: Ignatius Press, 2012), 25.

6. Mark and Jan Foreman interview with Natalie Stilwell, "Raising Creative Kids," So Goes the Future, June 24, 2021, YouTube video, https://www.youtube.com/watch?v=MkNqflcn3fg.

7. Jennifer Kolari, "Episode 11: When You Love Your Kid but Don't Like Them Very Much," *Connected Parenting* (podcast), April 25, 2019, https://www.connectedparenting.com/podcasts/when-you-love-your-kid-but-dont-like-them-very-much.

8. G. K. Chesterton, quoted in "Chesterton on Joy," The Society of G. K. Chesterton, accessed July 19, 2023, https://www.chesterton.org/chesterton-on-joy.

9. John Eldredge, *Get Your Life Back* (Nashville: Nelson Books, 2020), 31–32.

10: FAMILY VALUES INVENTORY

1. Mark Murphy, "Neuroscience Explains Why You Need to Write Down Your Goals If You Actually Want to Achieve Them," *Forbes*, April 15, 2018, https://www.forbes.com/sites/markmurphy/2018/04/15/neuroscience-explains-why-you-need-to-write-down-your-goals-if-you-actually-want-to-achieve-them/?sh=6b135a3c7905.